Montezuma

AND THE AZTECS

Mathilde Helly
Rémi Courgeon

A Henry Holt Reference Book

Henry Holt and Company

New York

A PICTURE IS WORTH A THOUSAND WORDS

Xun Zi (313-238 B.C.)

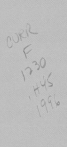

A Henry Holt Reference Book
Henry Holt and Company, Inc.
Publishers since 1866
115 West 18th Street
New York, New York 10011
Henry Holt® is a registered trademark
of Henry Holt and Company, Inc.

Library of Congress Cataloging-in-Publication Data
Helly, Mathilde.
Montezuma and the Aztecs/Mathilde Helly and
Rémi Courgeon.
p. cm.
—(W5 (who, what, where, when, and why) series)
(A Henry Holt reference book)
Includes bibliographical references and index.
1. Montezuma II, Emperor of Mexico, ca. 1480-1520.
2. Aztecs—Kings and rulers—Biography.
3. Aztecs—History. 4. Mexico—History—
Conquest, 1519-1540. I. Courgeon, Rémi. II. Title.
III. Series. IV. Series.
A Henry Holt reference book.
F1230.H45 1996   96-26389
972'.018—dc20   CIP

ISBN 0-8050-5060-4

Henry Holt books are available for special
promotions and premiums.
For details contact: Director, Special Markets.

Originally published in France in 1996 by
Editions Mango under the title *Cortés et son temps*.
First published in the United States in 1996
by Henry Holt and Company, Inc.

First American Edition—1996
Idea and series by Dominique Gaussen
American English translation by Hilary Davies
Typesetting by Jay Hyams and Christopher Hyams Hart

Printed in Italy by G. Canale & C. S.p.A. - Borgaro T.se - TURIN
All first editions are printed on acid-free paper. ∞

1 2 3 4 5 6 7 8 9 10

Mexican salad 4-5

Mexico seen from the thirteenth heaven 6-7

Mexica, the original Aztecs 8-9

The sun never goes anywhere alone 10-11

In Mexico blood transfusions kept the sun alive 12-13

The gods are like germs: they are countless, invincible, and hyperactive 14-15

Tenochtitlán, paradise 16-17

Memories of a great city 18-19

Eat your heart out 20-21

Portrait of Montezuma 22-23

After leading a full life, this is what an Aztec hoped for .24-25

How to climb the social ladder/How to tumble down the social ladder 26-27

External signs of internal wealth 28-29

The garland wars: they only sound pretty 30-31

The Aztecs never discovered the wheel, but their children played with it every day 32-33

In many cases, an Aztec sorcerer would have prescribed the same thing as your doctor 34-35

Did not exist in Spain/Did not exist in Mexico 36-37

Peyotl; or, taking trips without a horse 38-39

Who feeds those who feed the sun? 40-41

Gold is the sweat of the gods 42-43

In Mexico, people played basketball with their elbows and Parcheesi with beans 44-45

If this man is Quetzalcoatl . . . reading Aztec fortunes .46-47

Unequal in arms 48-49

Unfortunately for the Aztecs, at the beginning of the fifteenth century, the world became round . .50-51

With the Treaty of Tordesillas, the pope divides the world 52-53

Charles V, keeping the faith 54-55

Who had a taste for conquistadors? 56-57

Who won the first transatlantic race in history? 58-59

Hernán Cortés, just another hidalgo 60-61

How the Spanish discovered Mexico at a snail's pace 62-63

Captain Cortés and his crew are happy to welcome you aboard 64-65

How Cortés tore up his return ticket 66-67

Translation by Doña Marina 68-69

The route of conquest 70-71

Montezuma and Cortés: what were they thinking? 72-73

The most astonishing hostage-taking in history 74-75

Montezuma: murder or suicide? 76-77

The Spanish wept on the sad night 78-79

After three months of siege, fat rats look tasty 80-81

How a handful of Spaniards took on thousands of Aztecs 82-83

The sad end of the Aztec Empire 84-85

Charles V cuts short Cortés' calling card 86-87

The true brutality of the conquest and the Black Legend 88-89

The latest news from Europe 90-91

The Spanish departed, their god remained 92-93

It takes more than pencils to color in a culture 94-95

Index and credits 96

"When I think of the Aztecs, I think of cannibalism, bleeding hearts, and nice gold jewelry."

Megan, 11
student

"Didn't the Aztecs invent hot chocolate? Or was that chili con carne? I hope they ate beans."

Claire, 32
Tex-Mex waiter

"Bogus! The whole thing's bogus! The Aztecs built pyramids so high that no one could get down again. What a waste."

Bobby, 18
art student

"Everyone knows the Aztecs were a people descended from corn gods. I mean maize."

Marcia, 40
English teacher

"If you ask me, the Aztecs are relatives of the Olmecs and the Toltecs. Then there are the Tepanecs, right?"

Susan, 29
gym teacher

"They were a tribe of Indians that lived in old Mexico."

Michele, 14
student

SALAD

"I associate the Aztecs with huge pyramids, earthquakes, and the sun."

Oliver, 17
student

"I always confuse the Incas and the Aztecs. The Aztecs thought that if someone squinted it was a sign of beauty."

Bruce, 87
retired

"I think the Aztecs were Mayas, but descended from the Incas."

Robert, 42
sailor

"We learned about them in school: they lived in the New World, but it wasn't really so new."

Elly, 64
writer

"If Cortés hadn't come over, we'd eat a lot more chocolate and we wouldn't have to go to school because history would be shorter."

Bonnie, 15
student

"It was hot where the Aztecs lived so they ate chili. It was cold where the Incas lived so they had llamas. I'm not sure where the Mayas lived."

Dave, 35
nurse

People sometimes confuse the Aztecs, Mayas, and Incas, but these three pre-Columbian civilizations flourished at quite different times and in quite different places. The Mayan civilization is the oldest (toward the end of the third century A.D.). What we find remarkable about it are the gigantic temples, built of stone without any wooden frame. Their empire, based in the Yucatan, fell into decline at the beginning of the 1400s and was forced to share the peninsula with other warring tribes. When the Spanish arrived, they found many deserted cities, overgrown by the jungle. It was 1548 before the Yucatan was officially joined to New Spain, the land we now know as Mexico. Inca civilization was much more recent (beginning of the fifteenth century). These self-styled "children of the sun" kept llamas and lived on the high plateaus, sometimes 250 miles long, in the Andes. Their achievements are breathtaking: roads stretching from Quito in Peru to the Maule River in Chile, all provided with regular, properly equipped supply posts, and crossing rivers on suspended bridges; Machu Picchu, a citadel built at an altitude of nearly one and one-half miles. When the Spanish conquistador Francisco Pizarro reached the edges of this empire in 1531, it was at the height of its success. The modern-day descendants of the Incas are the Peruvians. In this book, however, we'll talk about the Aztecs.

5

Once upon a time there were two beings, a lord and a lady, who were halves of the same whole: Ometecuhtli and Omecihuatl. According to the Aztec creation myth, they had created themselves. They lived outside time and space, in other words, beyond Anahuac, at the summit of the world, in the thirteenth heaven. Here all men and gods were born. The gods had created the world, and in order to give birth to the sun, they had laid down their lives. And man was to perpetuate this sacrifice by in turn laying down his own life. The Aztecs believed that our world had been preceded by four previous universes, called the Four Suns. The first sun, the "Four Jaguars," had vanished after a great massacre during which mankind was devoured by jaguars. In the period of the second sun, the "Four Winds," man had been transformed into monkeys. The third sun, the "Four Rains," had been destroyed by a rain of fire. Finally, the fourth sun, the "Four Waters," had disappeared in a great flood that lasted 52 years. The Aztecs believed that our universe, called the "Four Earthquakes," would itself be destroyed by great seismic shocks. This catastrophe could come at any moment, but was especially possible at the conclusion of every 52-year cycle, which was the Aztec equivalent of our century. Only human sacrifice had any hope of maintaining the balance of the world by upholding the sun in its daily course and saving the world from chaos.

Mexico was a land of volcanoes, with northern deserts and southern tropics, but also with a temperate climate at higher altitudes. In the middle of the high central plateau, at 7,347 feet, lay the city of Tenochtitlán (modern-day Mexico City). It was from this plateau that the Aztecs (also known as the Mexica) dominated the valley.

MEXICO SEEN FROM THE THIRTEENTH HEAVEN

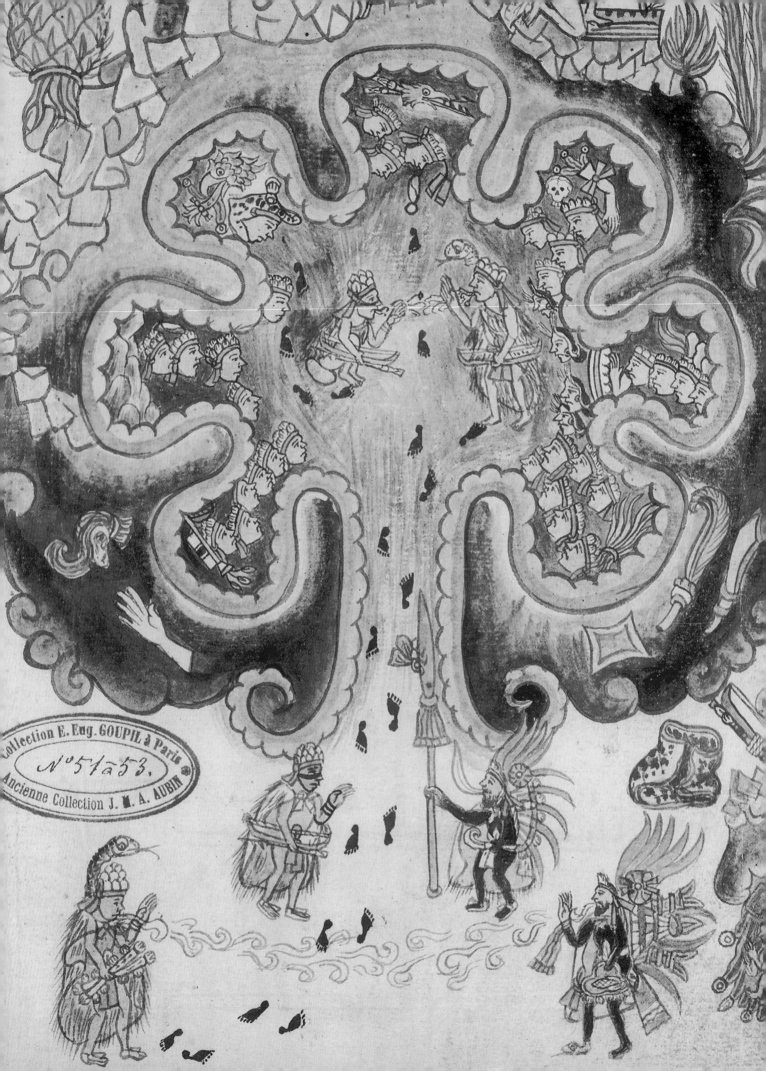

The origins of the Aztecs are unclear but dimly preserved in oral memories and written poems. There are few certainties for the historian, but marvelous opportunities for interpretation if you are interested in Mexico. History tells us that the Aztecs once lived in the faraway country of Aztlán in northwestern Mexico. They are thought to have arrived there in the middle of the second century. Probably they came from a region farther north. They spoke Nahuatl and were nomadic, living by fishing, hunting, and gathering; they wore animal skins and lived in caves. The local people called them Chichimecs, "sons of the dog," a reference to the fact that they lived as nomads.

They moved south when the city of Tula, founded in 856, was destroyed and abandoned by warring tribes in 1168. This city had been the center of the brilliant Toltec civilization, another people who spoke Nahuatl. One of the first stages of the great journey that was to take the Aztecs a century later to the Valley of Mexico was Chicómoztoc, meaning "place of seven caves." This legendary spot was the birthplace of the seven Nahua tribes that peopled the central plateau of Mexico: the Acolhua, Chalca, Chinampaneca, Culhua, Tepanec, Tlahuica, and Tlatepotzca. It was at this time that the Aztecs, previously indistinguishable from the other Nahua tribes, asserted their own tribal identity: they split off from the main body of tribes to leave Chicómoztoc and continue their journey.

According to legend, it was an oracle that prompted their move and sealed their fate: Huitzilopochtli, or "Hummingbird-on-the-Left," was at once man, god, and sorcerer. He had the power to change himself into an eagle or a hummingbird and also had the power of speech. He ordered the Aztecs to set off and conquer the world and pointed the way to central Mexico. Their route, after many resting places, led them to the borders of Lake Texcoco, in the middle of which lay an island covered with rocks and prickly-pear cactuses. Perched atop one of these cactus trees was a golden eagle devouring a snake (the eagle and snake are today Mexico's national emblem and appear on the Mexican flag). This was the long-awaited sign, first given to them five centuries before, through which the Aztec god indicated to his people that they should stop and found their city.

MEXICA, THE ORIGINAL AZTECS

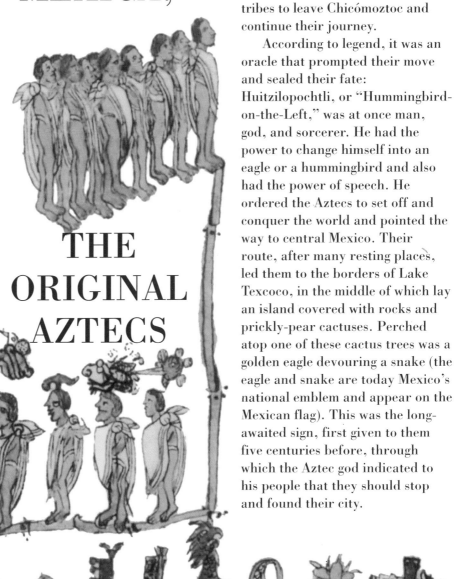

3

4

2

1

THE SUN NEVER GO

The Aztecs thought of life and death as parts of a single reality, very closely linked. Each person's destiny was part of an eternal cycle in which life gave way to death, which gave way to life again. If a man drowned, or was struck by lightning, or if he died as a result of a disease caused by water, he accompanied the god Tlaloc to a paradise where eternal rest and abundance awaited him. If he had been a warrior devoted to Huitzilopochtli, he was reborn out of the Underworld and journeyed daily with the sun from east to west. There were no ideas of moral reward,

retribution, or punishment. If the unfortunate ma had not been singled out either by Tlaloc or Huitzilopochtli, he disappeared forever into the great Void.

"This is what the ancients said about those who we to the palace of the sun"

(Bernardino de Sahag

1) "All men of courage and soldiers who died in war went ther They lived in the eastern part of the palace."

THE MOON
A fable tells how the gods mocked the moon and then threw a rabbit at its face.

ANYWHERE ALONE

2) *"In the morning, as the sun rose, they put on their armor and went to meet him, shouting and making a great noise."*

3) *"They then escorted him, putting on a mock battle as a sign of their happiness, to the high point of noon."*

4) *"The ancients also say that not only women who died in war, but also those who died in childbirth . . . also went to the palace of the sun, to live in the westerly part of the building, where the sun sets."*

5) *"The men left the sun in the company of the women and fanned out into the sky and its gardens, feeding on nectar until the following morning."*

6) *"The women in their turn led the sun to a bed made of rich feathers. They tended to him and vied with each other to entertain him."*

7) *"Then they left him as he retired, when the inhabitants of the Underworld would come to receive him and take him to where they lived."*

8) *"The ancients said that as night fell for us, day broke in the Underworld. The dead awoke from their sleep and surrounded the sun, while the women who had brought him there spread out over the earth, looking for spindles with which to spin, shuttles with which to weave, needles with which to sew, pin cushions, and all the tools necessary for sewing and making embroidery."*

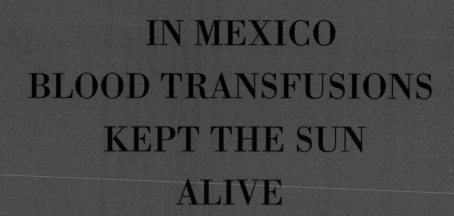

IN MEXICO
BLOOD TRANSFUSIONS
KEPT THE SUN
ALIVE

The people of Mexico were the "people of the sun." Their duty was to provide the sun with nourishment. The first words spoken to newborn boys as the umbilical cord was being cut were "This is your cradle, the place where you lay down your head. But your house is only a fleeting dwelling. Your real country is elsewhere . . . your purpose and your life is to give the sun the blood of your enemies to drink and to provide the earth, called Tlaltecutli, with the bodies of your adversaries to eat. As for your country, your inheritance and happiness, you will find them in heaven in the palace of the sun."

The sun, invoked as "the father and mother of mankind," was considered the supreme being. He was owed his ration of warm blood and beating hearts for the survival and well-being of the universe. Without this the world would be destroyed. These bloody offerings of human sacrifice were dedicated to all the gods whose lives affected man. The gods could die, but blood, also called "precious water," could bring them back to life. The god Huitzilopochtli protected the Mexica tribe in return for human blood. The Aztecs organized sacred wars, also called "garland wars," that were fought to capture prisoners to be sacrificed. Human sacrifice was the most important element in the ritual.

Rise, dress yourself, stand up,

Enjoy the beauty of this place:

The house of your mother and father, the sun.

There lie joy, pleasure, happiness.

Follow the road, follow your mother and father, the sun.

THE GODS ARE LIKE GERMS: THEY ARE COUNTLESS, INVINCIBLE, AND HYPERACTIVE

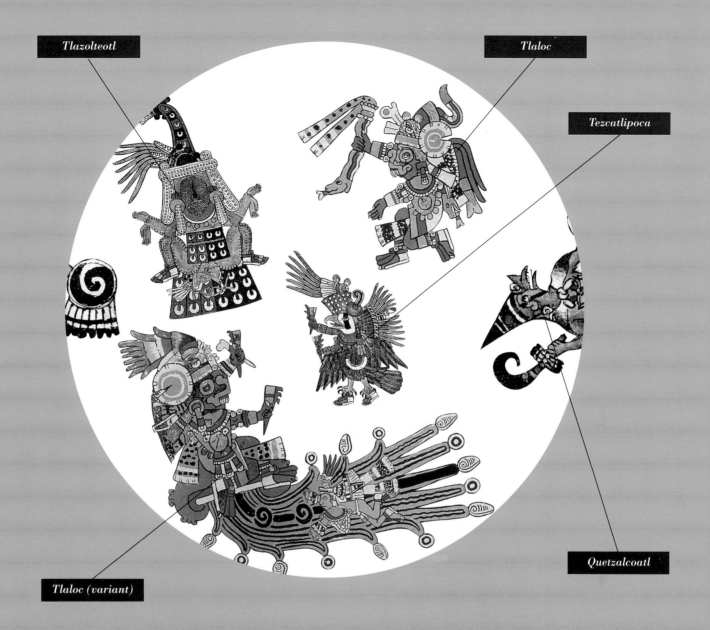

Tlazolteotl

Tlaloc

Tezcatlipoca

Quetzalcoatl

Tlaloc (variant)

Aztec religion was an open religion, without prejudice. The pantheon (house of the gods) welcomed an incalculable number of ancient and recent divinities, terrestrial and heavenly, gods of the lakes and gods of the earth. Whether they were Aztec or foreign, they corresponded to all forms of human endeavor, honored every social function, furthered every aspect of everyday life, and influenced all decisions. Religion gave meaning to both known and unknown phenomena.

At the beginning of time, a god and goddess brought four sons into the world: Xipe-Totec, Tezcatlipoca, Quetzalcoatl, and Huitzilopochtli. Xipe-Totec, "Our Lord the Flayed," shown wearing a human skin, was a god with many qualities, notably the ability to make plants regenerate with the seasons. Tezcatlipoca, the "Smoking Mirror, the mirror that has visions," with his distinctive attribute, an obsidian mirror, was the god of the north, of the night, of war, of the winds, and protected young warriors. Huitzilopochtli, the "Hummingbird-on-the-Left," the "warrior raised up from the earth," was the god of war and the noonday sun. The supreme god of the Aztecs, he demanded the "precious water" of human blood. Quetzalcoatl, the "Feathered Serpent," symbol of Nahua wisdom and of religion itself, of art, of writing, of high civilization, was the incarnation of the wind, the sun, and the planet Venus. In the mists of time, he had also been a rich head of state, a man of generosity, beauty, and gentleness. But at a certain moment, he had been forced to leave his kingdom and journey to exile in the east. The myth said that he had promised that one day he would return to reclaim his possessions.

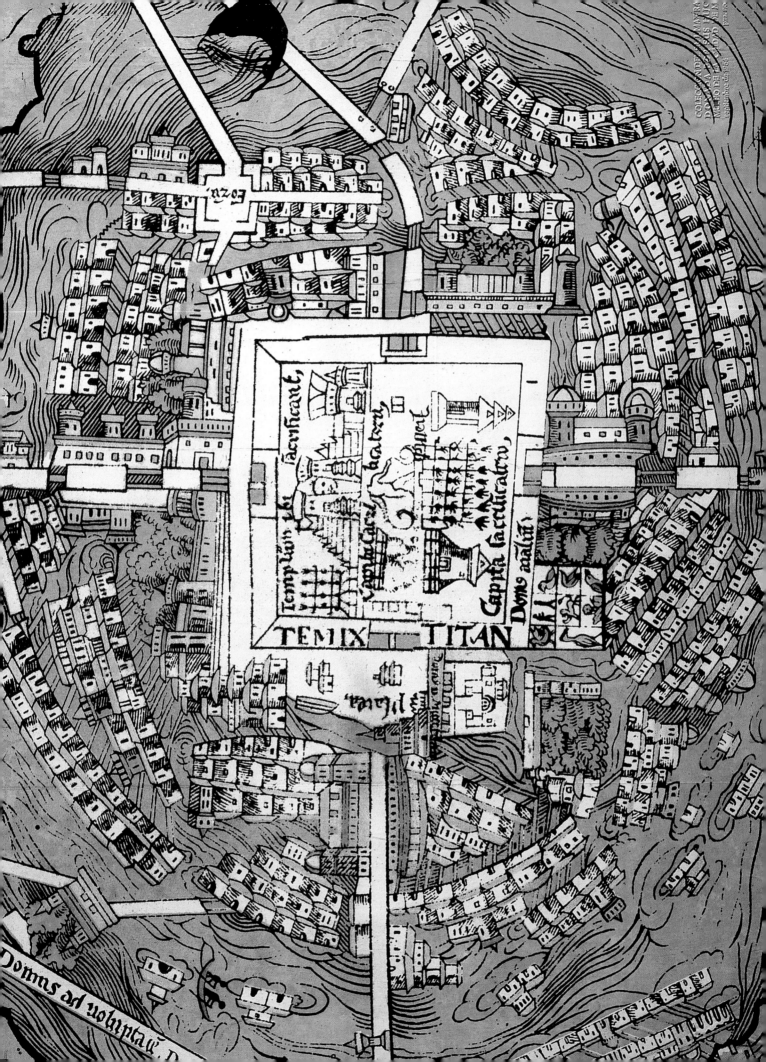

INZOZ

Templum ubi sacrificant,

Capita sacrificatorum,

Domus animalium

TEMIX ✝ TITAN

Fisicra,

TENOCHTITLÁN, PARADISE

Built over four square miles, the city of Tenochtitlán (today's Mexico City) was home to between 80,000 and 100,000 families, roughly 500,000 inhabitants—about 1,300 people per square mile. (The population of Mexico City in 1900 was only half as many people.) This densely inhabited city began on an island in Lake Texcoco, and that one island gradually swallowed up other smaller ones and was linked to the mainland by three causeways and roads.

The Aztecs built new islands on mounds of earth placed in the silty waters of the lake. The Aztecs paddled dugout canoes up and down the grid pattern of canals and past the island gardens. Pedestrians used beaten-earth pavements and drawbridges to reach the blocks of houses, simple rectangular constructions with no windows facing the street. The life of the Mexica was turned inward, toward hidden courtyards. The capital was divided into four administrative sections, each with its own temple, chief of staff, *telpochcalli* (military academies), and *calmécac* (seminaries), which were places of learning and also of worship. Large buildings dotted the city at carefully chosen intervals, and the central square housed both the market and the palace of Montezuma.

This palace contained the imperial suites, the high courts, both civil and criminal, the special tribunal where high-ranking officials were tried, the war council, the treasury, and rooms that were used as a prison. And then there were the temples, like that of Huitzilopochtli, the pyramid of which was 98 feet high. It rested on a rectangular base 328 feet long and 262 feet wide and was made up of four or five parts. On one side, a great staircase of 114 steps rose up almost vertically before being topped by a platform surrounded by the sanctuaries of Tlaloc and Huitzilopochtli, in front of each of which stood a sacrificial altar; 300 feet to the east of this building stood the temple of Quetzalcoatl, a cylindrical structure resting on a pyramidal base. The Mexica moved about their city day and night.

By day, they shopped at the markets, busied themselves in their homes, kept up the streets, collected drinking water from the huge stone-and-cement aqueduct. The night they reserved for more important visits, banquets, and the many rituals that went to make up their society.

On the great square of Tenochtitlán the merchants held sway. There were purveyors of birds, turkeys, rabbit, and venison, merchants selling beans and other vegetables, cotton, salt, and wood, and trappers selling skins of jaguar, lion, otter, jackal, and deer; there were cutlers making obsidian knives and potters turning pots of all sizes; sellers of honey and "reeds that smell of liquidambar [the scented sap of a native North American tree] and are full of tobacco"; sellers of "small cakes made from a sort of weed that they get out of the lagoon and that curdles and forms a kind of bread that tastes rather like cheese." Lastly there were the gold and silver merchants and dealers in precious stones, feathers, fabrics, and embroidery.

The headdress makers, jewelers, stonecutters, and silver- and goldsmiths were high-status artisans. Feathers had a religious significance, so working with them was considered one of the highest arts. The ceremonial objects— headdresses, crowns, jewelry, shields—were masterpieces of mosaiclike inlay. Gold- and

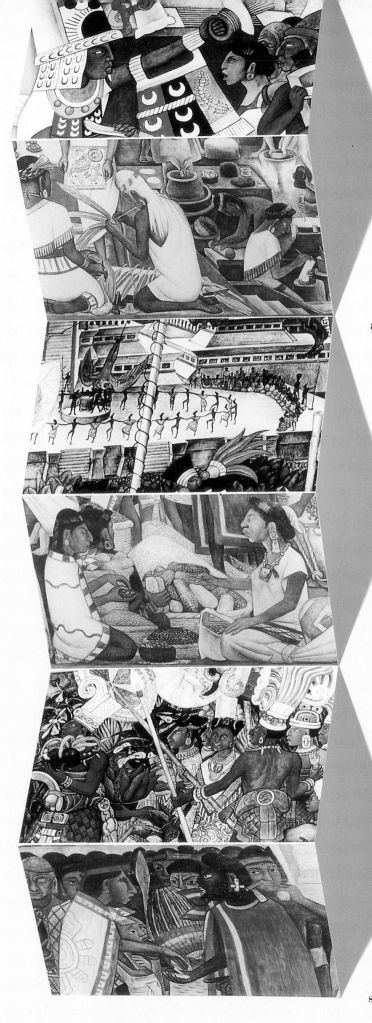

silverwork had reached a high level; the mines of these precious metals provided an inexhaustible supply of minerals for the creation of ear and nose rings, necklaces, pectorals, bracelets, and anklets. The people who cast, beat, and worked metals did not sell their work: they left that to the merchants, who used a system of barter. Jewelry-making, also highly regarded as a noble skill, consisted of cutting, polishing, and mounting emerald, turquoise, and coral for ceremonial insignia, such as the chin ornaments for men, which they wore just beneath their lower lip. And then there was stonemasonry, which entailed quarrying, cutting, and sculpting stone, mainly for religious purposes: statues of gods, capitals, and bas-reliefs, but also stone funerary masks, sometimes inlaid with turquoise, obsidian, and garnet.

Each group of artisans had its own quarter in the city, its own gods and rites. The guilds were exclusive, a fact that often reflected their ethnic origins: for instance, all the evidence suggests that the headdress-makers came from a tribe living in Amantlan, a village that had been swallowed up in Tenochtitlán. No doubt this is why the trade was passed down from generation to generation. They worked either at home or in the imperial workshops. Most of the objects they made were related to beliefs, traditions, or social hierarchies.

The high priest bore a large ceremonial knife made of gilt flint. When the victim's heart had been extracted, the victim was rolled down the stairs.

At the top of the 114 steps that led to the teocalli ("the house of god"), the priests offered the gods what was most precious to them: human blood.

EAT YOUR HEART OUT

Human sacrifice was one of the sacred rites of the Aztecs. The "garland wars" and the raids carried out by the imperial tax collectors were intended to procure the necessary human flesh for this ceremony. Very strict rules determined just who could be sacrificed. You did not sacrifice your fellow countrymen, strangers, or the sick. The victim had to come from a nearby nation and be healthy, with proven warrior abilities. Once caught, the future victim was kept in prison for a while to be prepared for the fate awaiting him or her. To be sacrificed was an honor, because it guaranteed perpetual happiness.

To glorify the god Tezcatlipoca, a young man, chosen for his skills, physical prowess, and artistic gifts, was showered with favors for a whole year. Young girls were sacrificed to the goddess Xilonen. The day before the sacrifice, the face of the girl was painted with yellow and red, and she was decorated with paper crowns and large necklaces. She sang and danced all night long in front of the temple, surrounded by women similarly made up. When the moment arrived for the sacrifice, the victim was led to the top of the temple and met by six priests, four to hold the victim's feet and hands, another to hold his or her head, and the sixth to perform the sacrifice. The victim was thrown on his or her back over the sacrifice stone, and the sixth priest would cut open the chest, extract the victim's heart, and offer it, still beating, to the sun.

Then the victim's body would be thrown down the temple steps. The body was cut up: the skin, stuffed with cotton, went to decorate the facade of the palace where the priests lived; the right thigh went to the emperor; the head was impaled on a stake; the blood was smeared on the statues of the temple. The rest was eaten by the family of the man who had captured the victim or was thrown to the wild beasts kept in the palace. Sometimes several victims were sacrificed, killed one by one by the same group of priests.

The smell of decaying flesh and coagulated blood was masked by copal incense.

The moments leading up to the sacrifice and its ceremony varied from one god to another. To celebrate the fire god, the people fasted for four days before dancing to the sound of drums, in costumes resembling the clothing and ornaments of the god. At the end, "They cut the heads off a great number of quail and spilled their blood before the idol of the god. Some pierced their ears, others their tongue, with maguey* thorns and pushed twigs through the holes to maintain the flow of blood"; a kind of self-mutilation. At other festivals, edible offerings were made: maize, beans, cooked tamales (*tamalli*, in Nahuatl), bread in the shape of butterflies, and others.

* Maguey, or agave, is a plant with large leaves that yields a sweet juice that the Aztecs fermented into a drink called pulque.

PORTRAIT OF MONTEZUMA

Montezuma II (his Aztec name was Moctezuma) was the absolute monarch of the Aztecs, the spiritual, military, and civil leader of his people. For a hundred years, the Aztec throne had been hereditary, and Montezuma II had come to the throne, or *icpalli* (a legless chair; its base rested on the floor), in 1503. In that year, the kings of Texcoco and Tlacopán (Tacuba) had placed a crown of gold and turquoise on his head and had fixed heavy earrings on his ears. He had then climbed the steps of the temple dedicated to Huitzilopochtli, his ears, legs, and arms stuck with agave thorns; once at the top, he had sacrificed several quail on the altar; then with a gold incense burner he had waved incense toward the four corners of the earth to symbolize his power and authority.

Surrounded by his two wives, his many concubines, and more than five hundred noblemen and attendants, he lived in a vast palace that could be reached on foot or by boat. The palace complex encompassed several buildings grouped around internal courtyards and gardens. The treasures in this Mexican Eden were carefully hidden behind walls: inside were the rarest of flowers, splashing fountains, aviaries and zoos with fine examples of birds and animals. There were about one hundred apartments, with walls richly decorated with red and green marble and jade, colored tapestries, ceilings of sculpted wood, and cypress floors. Montezuma's rooms were on an upper floor, near the suites reserved for the kings of allied peoples and other associates. Perfume burners gave off a delicate scent everywhere. Meals followed an elaborate pattern: the emperor, dressed in clothes of precious fabrics and wearing golden sandals, selected the dishes he wanted from among more than three hundred; these were then heated on a brazier. Served by four beautiful women, he ate alone, seated on an *icpalli* in front of a low table. As befitted a great lover of amusements and games, he would listen to flutes, drums, and two-toned gongs or would call in his jesters so that he could be amused by their antics or be lulled by poems recited or sung. He liked to finish his supper with a cup of cocoa and a pipe of tobacco.

Montezuma was a majestic person whom the ordinary Aztecs did not dare look upon, on pain of death. If they encountered his procession, they had to lower their head and give way or take another route. The empire was still a loose assembly of peoples, a confederation of city states. The most powerful of these—Tenochtitlán, Texcoco, and Tlacopán—formed a Triple Alliance, headed by Montezuma. These three cities

The palace of Montezuma

covered a wide zone of influence, but Tenochtitlán was the most important. Mexican territory had little uniformity. Montezuma was at pains to unify it by conquering the surrounding peoples, who were constantly at war. The subjugated cities were forced to pay regular tribute, a situation that made many of them deeply unhappy.

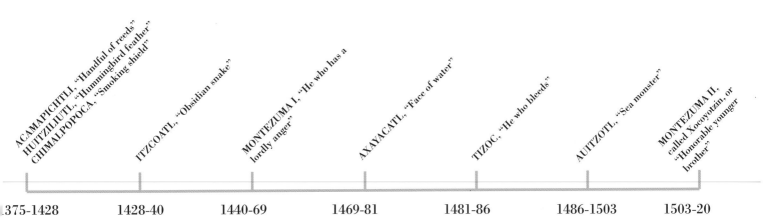

ACAMAPICHTLI, "Handful of reeds"
HUITZILIUTL, "Hummingbird feather"
CHIMALPOPOCA, "Smoking shield"

ITZCOATL, "Obsidian snake"

MONTEZUMA I, "He who has a lordly anger"

AXAYACATL, "Face of water"

TIZOC, "He who bleeds"

AUITZOTL, "Sea monster"

MONTEZUMA II, called Xocoyotzin, or "Honorable younger brother"

1375-1428   1428-40   1440-69   1469-81   1481-86   1486-1503   1503-20

Birth in Aztec culture was an extremely important and propitious moment. The midwife, who was absolutely crucial, presided over the birth by following a complex ritual of coded gestures and words. She told the child, "You are a warrior, a *quecholli* bird," if it was a boy; or, "You must become like the ash of the hearth," if it was a girl. Then the baby was presented to the community, before being showered with presents. After this, the sorcerer was sent for; he determined what sign the child had been born under.

Only then was the child named: the midwife washed the baby and gave him or her a name. The ceremony finished with a family feast. The education of children was strict, with harsh punishments: being scratched with agave thorns, or being forced to inhale red pimento or dried garlic steam. Coming of age for boys—indicated by putting on the loincloth called a *maxtlatl*—was at age 13. Until then, fathers taught their sons how to carry water and wood and how to fish. Girls helped their mothers to keep the house and weave. Children were then sent to a *calmécac* or *telpochcalli* to finish their education. The *calmécac* ("house of tears") was a kind of boardingschool academy for boys considered to be a temple under the guidance of Quetzalcoatl.

Here boys prepared to become priests or take on high offices of state. The education given by the priests was that of "good manners,"

learning rituals and the reading of manuscripts. Life was austere, and the students, mostly the sons of high-ranking officials, had to prove they were capable of self-denial: speeches learned by heart, mastery of rhetoric, self-sacrifice. The students in *telpochcalli* ("houses of youth") learned military duties. Their days were spent studying martial arts and strategy, but also public works and agriculture; in the evening they danced and sang. When they were about age 20, they left the monastery or college, often to marry. Marriages were arranged by the parents through marriage brokers, often older women who tied together the dress of the fiancée and the cloak of the young man in the presence of the families; then they shared a dish of tamales: this was the marriage ceremony.

After four days of prayer, there was a big feast. Polygamy was widespread, especially among the more well to do. Adultery was punishable by death. After death, the Aztecs were buried—if they had been singled out by Tlaloc—or cremated. When the cremation was over, the ashes were gathered and placed in a funerary urn that was then buried in the garden. Warriors hoped to be reincarnated as a hummingbird, like Huitzilopochtli, the warrior god.

AFTER LEADING A FULL LIFE, THIS IS WHAT AN AZTEC

HOPED FOR

HOW TO CLIMB THE SOCIAL LADDER

The nobility, called *tecuhtli*, were not the richest Aztecs, but they composed the most envied class. It is true that they did possess wealth, paid no taxes, and had a privileged place at certain ceremonies; but at the same time they had to protect their fellow citizens, give alms to the elderly, and keep up to date the register of common land belonging to the state, but farmed by the people of each *calpulli* (the group of houses of a hereditary clan), since all land was collective, and the product of labor was distributed to the population. Nevertheless, it was really only prestige that mattered to this class, and to become a *cacique* (important person, dignitary) among caciques, you had to earn it. The best way to climb the social ladder was a military career or performance of an administrative or religious office. It was possible to get these honorific titles by capturing four enemy soldiers, even if you were only in the rank and file. The gateway to power and command was thus opened. In the eleventh month of the year, the emperor distributed rewards and honors. The deserving soldier thus owed his rise to war.

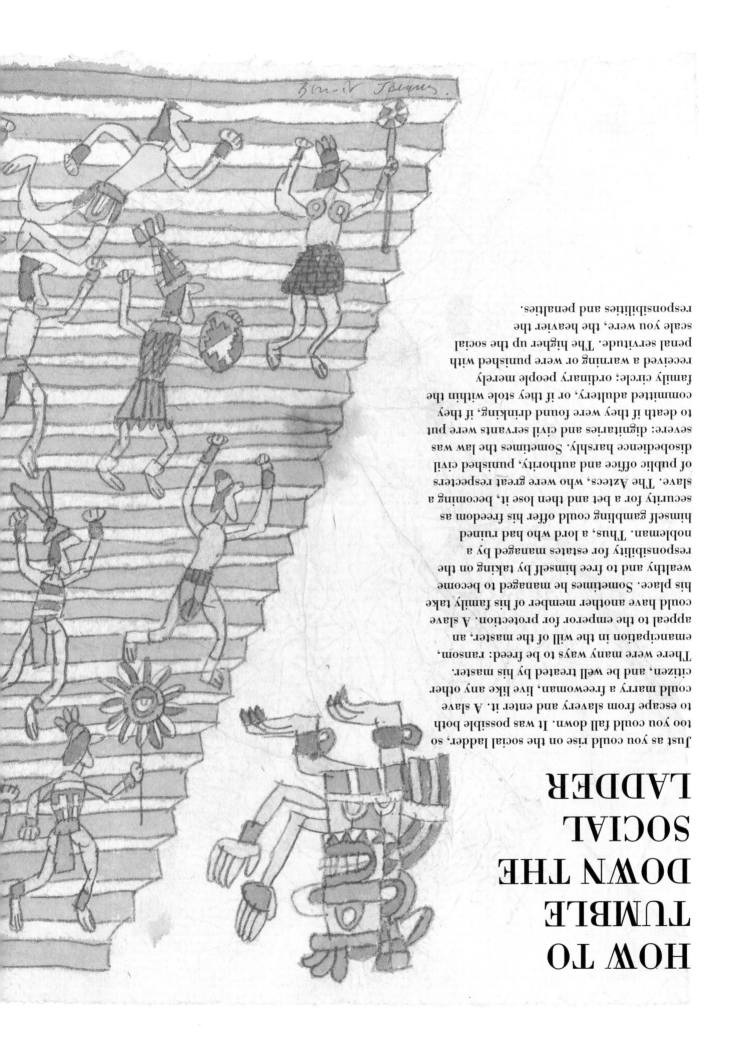

HOW TO TUMBLE DOWN THE SOCIAL LADDER

Just as you could rise on the social ladder, so too you could fall down. It was possible both to escape from slavery and enter it. A slave could marry a freewoman, live like any other citizen, and be well treated by his master. There were many ways to be freed: ransom, emancipation in the will of the master, an appeal to the emperor for protection. A slave could have another member of his family take his place. Sometimes he managed to become wealthy and to free himself by taking on the responsibility for estates managed by a nobleman. Thus, a lord who had ruined himself gambling could offer his freedom as security for a bet and then lose it, becoming a slave. The Aztecs, who were great respecters of public office and authority, punished civil disobedience harshly. Sometimes the law was severe: dignitaries and civil servants were put to death if they were found drinking, if they committed adultery, or if they stole within the family circle; ordinary people merely received a warning or were punished with penal servitude. The higher up the social scale you were, the heavier the responsibilities and penalties.

EXTERNAL SIGNS OF INTERNAL WEALTH

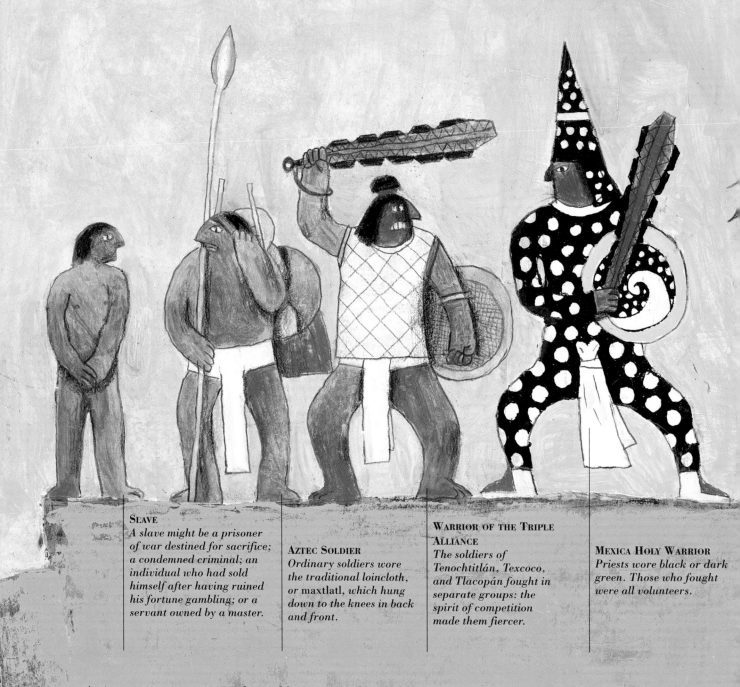

SLAVE
A slave might be a prisoner of war destined for sacrifice; a condemned criminal; an individual who had sold himself after having ruined his fortune gambling; or a servant owned by a master.

AZTEC SOLDIER
Ordinary soldiers wore the traditional loincloth, or maxtlatl, which hung down to the knees in back and front.

WARRIOR OF THE TRIPLE ALLIANCE
The soldiers of Tenochtitlán, Texcoco, and Tlacopán fought in separate groups: the spirit of competition made them fiercer.

MEXICA HOLY WARRIOR
Priests wore black or dark green. Those who fought were all volunteers.

As it came into contact with neighboring peoples, Aztec society gradually changed, becoming aristocratic, imperialistic, and hierarchical. Within this society, people usually did not hesitate to show off their wealth or station. In fact, an individual's position in society could be seen at a glance.

The *tilmatli*, or cloak, made of agave and cotton fiber and put on over the head, was the most popular garment. Ordinary citizens wore very plain garments while the clothes of dignitaries were quite fancy. Each article of plumage, each headdress, each emblem or shield commemorated a particular deed and symbolized the divine power of the individual and reminded others of the honors due that person.

JAGUAR WARRIOR OF THE TRIPLE ALLIANCE
The "Jaguar Warriors," soldiers of Tezcatlipoca, wore a suit of real jaguar skin.

MEXICA CAPTAIN
In times of war, clothing like that of this captain was padded to better protect against enemy arrows.

MEXICA GENERAL
Military leaders formed the highest rank of the hierarchical society. They fought alongside the great priests and high functionaries of Mexico.

MEXICA EMPEROR
The emperor, or tlatoani ("he who commands"), was the only person allowed to wear a turquoise nose ornament. He was the commander of all the Aztec armies.

Anyone who falsely wore these colors was put to death. Everybody had to uphold the honor of his position in society, at the risk of losing everything. These external signs of wealth, which were sometimes accompanied by considerable material riches—houses, many servants, grain and gold reserves— were the result of military and moral prowess. Only priests, living in austerity, and merchants, who did not want others to know how rich they were for fear of offending those of higher social status, avoided outward displays of wealth. The Aztecs believed that the rich came by their wealth because of merit, and they did not honor people only because their pockets were full of gold.

Some Aztec wars were not real wars that killed people, but wars that were called "garlanded." This does not mean that they were less horrible, only that they were agreed upon beforehand and had rules.

The Aztec Empire was ruled by the kings of the cities of the Triple Alliance: Tenochtitlán, Texcoco, and Tlacopán. They intimidated the neighboring towns in the hope of subjugating them and thereby gaining better control over them. They were suspicious of any town that proclaimed its sovereignty and resisted their rule. The kings were always on the alert for a reason to declare war on such towns. For example, an attack on a traveling merchant was always a good excuse. The dispute began with

conversations and ended in negotiations. A series of complex rules was respected throughout the bargaining, with the aim of getting the coveted town to submit without fighting. If it allied itself with the empire, it was exempt from paying tribute; all the townspeople had to do was agree by offering some kind of gift in the form of gold, precious stones, feathers, or cloaks, and to accept the god Huitzilopochtli as the equal of their local gods. However, if, after the twenty days reflection allowed by the imperial ambassadors, the town refused to submit, its inhabitants were again threatened: the lord of the town was put to death, and its noblemen were punished or sacrificed to the gods. The ambassadors would then withdraw, giving the town

THE GARLAND WARS: THEY ONLY SOUND PRETTY

another twenty days to think things over. If the town gave in, the negotiations would stop: the town's inhabitants were then forced to pay an annual tribute to the emperor, with whom they were now allied. If the town continued to resist, there were more threats: the surrounding province would be laid waste, prisoners taken as slaves, and tribute demanded. With each warning, the ambassadors would don their arms and shields "so that no one could say they had been conquered by treason." If, when this ultimatum expired, no agreement had been reached, war was declared.

The opposing sides first organized their forces. Spying was the rule. Secret agents were dressed like the local people. The Aztecs were experts at camouflage and ambush. Any double-crossing was punishable by death. Then, on the appointed day, the imperial procession set off toward the town to be conquered: priests, statues of the gods, captains, and soldiers followed a day behind.

Then it was war. Accompanied by shouts of encouragement and military orders, men were pitted against one another in hand-to-hand fighting in which the soldiers tried not so much to kill as to capture victims for sacrifice. To honor the fight and be sure of victory, the first captives were sacrificed at the feet of idols that had been carried into enemy territory. The town was conquered when the aggressor entered the temple precinct of the local god and set it alight. The battle was often short.

Finally the ambassadors settled the nature of the tribute to be paid—food, merchandise, jewelry, services—and demanded that the town recognize Huitzilopochtli as supreme god and Tenochtitlán as sovereign city. However, although a tax had to be paid, the town kept its culture and institutions.

The rules, technique, and tribute were all very fitting for such ceremonial disputes: the "garland wars," not pretty, indeed.

THE AZTECS NEVER DISCOVERED THE WHEEL, BUT THEIR CHILDREN PLAYED WITH IT EVERY DAY

Toys with wheels have been found in tombs from the period of the Aztecs, but the Aztecs made no use of the wheel in their everyday lives. Of course, they had no horses and no draft animals, so they had no need for carts, chariots, or wagons to carry them from one place to another. In Mexican territory, the only power was manpower, but they did have ways of reducing distances. How long do you think it took Montezuma, living in Tenochtitlán, to find out what was happening on the gulf coast, nearly 200 miles away? One day. You're astonished? Such feats were made possible by

The Aztecs used wheels only in decorations and toys, such as this clay dog.

using teams of relay runners. In reality, every journey was filled with risk and uncertainty. Trade and commerce were conducted according to rules, and custom demanded that strangers should be treated with hospitality. Even so, once they were on foreign territory—which usually meant enemy territory—merchants were often attacked. Most merchants exported manufactured products and imported luxury goods. This was not made easier by the distances involved, especially when the merchant

had to carry his own provisions as well as his merchandise, which also included his payment. Since different currencies did not exist, the merchant would be paid in other goods and merchandise. Raw goods were used for manufacturing in Tenochtitlán. Some of these came from the tribute offered by subjugated provinces, which almost certainly had to pay the cost of transport. Such difficulties were just as true of military campaigns. Rations could be transported only by using a system of relay supply posts. Some were stored in the granaries of the tributary cities, which provided a more regular supply for troops. While it is true that the Aztecs did not have horses or the wheel, they managed to get around. And during this period European roads were often little more than muddy tracks about three feet wide, intended for riders, but frequently overrun by herds of animals, so travelers often created quicker routes for themselves. The only important progress in Europe in the sixteenth century was the setting up of a system of stage posts, manned by postmasters who were expected to provide a fresh horse to riders carrying the proper documents. Distances of up to 60 miles a day could be covered in this way; Rome to Madrid could be done in 27 days. The postal system had been born. But this was only a copy of the ingenious system of transport that had been used for decades in Mexico.

Aztec merchants, burdened with their goods, on the road to a town. The footprints indicate their movement.

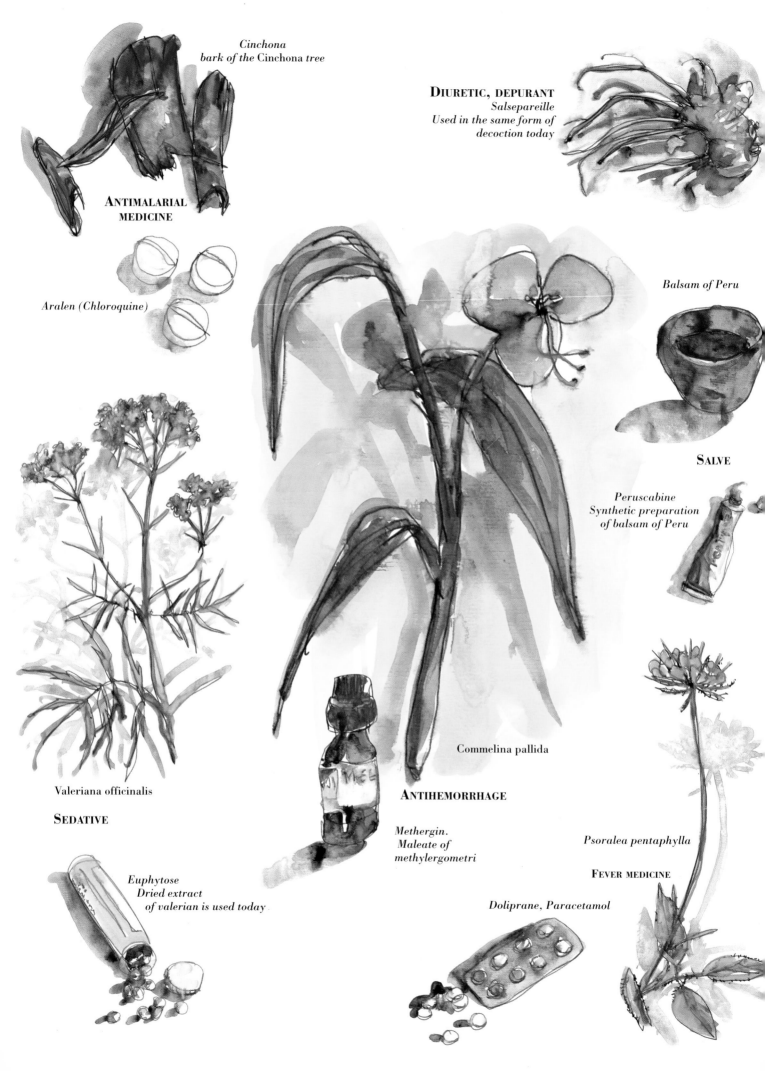

Cinchona
bark of the Cinchona tree

ANTIMALARIAL
MEDICINE

Aralen (Chloroquine)

DIURETIC, DEPURANT
Salsepareille
Used in the same form of
decoction today

Balsam of Peru

SALVE

Peruscabine
Synthetic preparation
of balsam of Peru

Commelina pallida

ANTIHEMORRHAGE

Methergin.
Maleate of
methylergometri

Psoralea pentaphylla

FEVER MEDICINE

Valeriana officinalis

SEDATIVE

Euphytose
Dried extract
of valerian is used today

Doliprane, Paracetamol

IN MANY CASES, AN AZTEC SORCERER WOULD HAVE PRESCRIBED THE SAME THING AS YOUR DOCTOR

Illness is especially worrying when it cannot be treated. Even today, we face many questions concerning diseases. In sophisticated laboratories, scientists probe the human body and nature, trying to find remedies and vaccines for people whose future has been made uncertain by illness. The Aztecs had found their own answers to some of these questions. Their medicine was based for the most part on religion and magic. They believed that illness was caused by the magical entry of a foreign body into the organism. They used the skills of women healers called *tetlacuicuilique* ("those who draw out stones"), *tetlanocuilanque* ("those who draw out worms from the teeth"), and *teixocuilanque* ("those who draw out worms from the eyes"). They also thought that some illnesses had been sent by the gods, in which case the disease could be cured by the gods who had sent it or by other gods. When suitable, the Aztecs also made vows or offerings to Tlaloc, the god of the mountains, because he was responsible for sicknesses caused by the cold, skin diseases, ulcers, leprosy, and swelling. Or they visited sorcerers. Aztec sorcerers diagnosed illnesses by examining how grains of maize fell when thrown onto a piece of cloth. Or they used pieces of rope or smeared tobacco on their hands and measured the left arm of the patient with the palm of their right hand. They also used the hallucinogenic drug peyotl, and invocations and magic were also helpful to believers. In fact, because of the practice of human sacrifice, Aztec sorcerers were quite familiar with human anatomy. They could set fractures, carry out bleedings, use steam baths, and apply plasters to abscesses. Most of all, they knew how to prepare medications from plants and prescribe infusions. They knew the properties of plants and minerals and even attributed certain healing qualities to animals and stones.

DID NOT EXIST IN SPAIN

RUBBER
They played with balls "made from resin or heavy rubber, called *ulli*, which are very light and bounce like an inflated bladder."

MAIZE
Aztec riddles: "What thing is to be found everywhere leaning over us?" Answer: "Ears of corn, which bend over when they dry." "What's an old woman with white hay hair standing next to the front door?" "It's the stack of corn."

TURKEY

JAGUAR
The Aztecs considered their kings to be descendants of Tezcatlipoca, the jaguar god, to whom they sacrificed a young man trained "to play the flute perfectly, and to wear flowers and fragrant reeds . . . he was brought up to smoke gracefully and to appreciate the fragrance of the flowers, and to bear himself like the great and the royal."

ARTICHOKE

PUMA
The puma, or *cuitlamiztli*, "according to what they say, it is a wolf that eats deer, chickens, and ewes; when it catches a deer, it eats its fill and can sleep for two or three days without hunting."

AVOCADOS

PELICAN
"To catch the pelican, the hunters lie in wait for two or three days, and on the third, they catch it. . . . If on the fourth day they have not caught it before sundown, they regard themselves as beaten and know that they must die because the time that they should have taken to kill it has run out."

TOMATOES

TAPIR
"It is a large animal, larger than a big cow, with a big head, long muzzle, and broad ears. It has large teeth and molars. . . . The meat is edible and tastes like all kinds of animals, from bird even to man."

THE HUMMINGBI
"In this land the are very tin birds that loo more like blu flies than bird. The a man species them. The have small, blac very fine beaks lif needles . . . they fee on nectar like bees.

COCOA
The Aztecs made cocoa (or cacao) into a drink by drying the beans, pounding them into a paste, and making little cakes. They then shook the cakes with water in a gourd until it frothed. A visitor later noted that the Mexicans "appear to diminish when they do not have that drink".

DID NOT EXIST IN MEXICO

WOOL
The various regions and countries of Europe specialized in agricultural productions and animal husbandry. Spain was then known for its wool, an industry given great support by Ferdinand and Isabella.

LINEN

HORSE
"Do you know, sirs," said Cortés, "these Indians seem to be extremely afraid of horses and believe that they go to war of their own accord, like bombards!"

SAILING SHIPS
Sailing ships did not exist in Mexico. The native boats were made of hollowed-out tree trunks. Many of these could hold 40 or 50 Indians standing up.

MONEY
"We saw other merchants who . . . sold grains of gold just like it comes out of the mines. They were contained in little tubes made with goosefeathers from that country... Buying and selling was done according to the thickness and length of these tubes: this was worth so much material, so many cocoa beans."

Cows, pigs, and goats were unknown in the New World. The Aztecs needed no draft animals, and the dog and turkey were their only domestic animals. The Aztecs learned animal husbandry with the arrival of the Spanish.

WRITTEN ALPHABET
The Aztecs used a system of symbols, or glyphs, instead of a written alphabet. Hence the importance of spoken commentaries "which have been passed down to you by the men and women of ancient times; they have been assimilated into our very breasts and entrails."

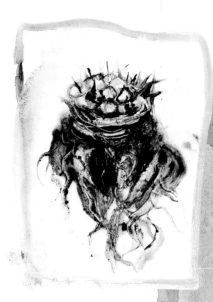

PEYOTL; OR, TAKING TRIPS WITHOUT A HORSE

The Aztecs were not likely to travel by horse: they didn't have any! They traveled in their minds with the help of certain hallucinogenic drugs. What were they for? To feel strong before a battle and to overcome fear, hunger, and thirst in times of famine or war. But feelings of well-being were not necessarily guaranteed. In fact, what they most hoped for was prophetic visions that were supposed to reveal the future. Drugs were not taken casually; they were shared at the beginning of meals, at banquets given by merchants before a journey, or by priests at sacrifices. The flesh of the peyotl (also known as peyote, peyotl is a kind of cactus found in North Mexico), when dried and taken in large doses, induced visual hallucinations of brilliant colors. These were very violent and were characterized by laughter, then tears; they could sometimes end in death. In order to intensify the effects, which could last three days, people fasted before taking the drug. The "sacred mushrooms," or *teonanacatl*, produced similar hallucinations. "Some saw that they were about to die, and wept; others believed they were being devoured by wild animals, and others saw themselves capturing enemies on the field of battle, or becoming rich, or great slave owners. And there were yet others who thought they had been accused of adultery and were to have their head smashed . . . when the madness caused by these mushrooms had worn off, they talked among themselves about the visions they'd had" (Bernardino de Sahagún).

The Aztecs were much aware of the bad effects of drunkenness; the only alcoholic drinks known to them, *pulque* and *octli* (rather like cider), were forbidden. An ordinary member of the public was punished severely if found drinking; priests and officials were immediately condemned to death. But in their wisdom the authorities allowed old men to drink, since their advanced age meant they were unlikely to become violent, and also because it was one of the few pleasures left to them in life.

WHO FEEDS THOSE WHO FEED THE SUN

?

Aztec food was varied and plentiful. It was most often boiled or grilled and was seasoned with spices and chili peppers. The main meal was eaten early in the afternoon and was usually followed by a short siesta. This meal consisted of tortillas and beans with tomatoes and peppers. The morning and evening meals were frugal. After several hours of work, the people were happy to eat a dish of boiled maize with honey or spiced with peppers, called *atolli*. For supper, they ate cold food. Maize was the staple, eaten boiled, as tortillas, or as tamales. Tamales stuffed with such delicacies as snails were enjoyed by high-ranking officials and the rich. Beans came a close second as the most popular food, followed by tomatoes, peppers, squash, and amaranth and sage seeds in a soup. The Aztecs rounded out their diet with fish, shellfish, frogs, and shrimp from the lake, many kinds of waterfowl, such as ducks, sweet potatoes brought from the coastal regions, turkeys, dogs (the meat of a kind of small dog was very popular), weasel, rabbit, pheasant, rattlesnake, iguana, insects, algae, and various worms. The common people of the Aztec Empire ate as well or better than the peasants in Europe at that time. For dessert, they had many kinds of fruit, maize tortillas, and cocoa sweetened with honey or vanilla, a drink especially appreciated by the aristocracy. Officials liked to smoke a reed or clay pipe during their meals; these were richly decorated and filled with tobacco, charcoal, and spices. Sometimes they ate and drank till dawn. Because of their ingenious irrigation system, the Aztecs were able to cultivate their land continuously. But they experienced periods of famine and scarcity, especially in June and July between harvests. A swarm of locusts or an explosion in the rodent population, too heavy rain or snowfalls, could destroy whole harvests in a few days, even hours. Gathering was a way of surviving if the emperor did not open his grain stores or distribute tamales and *atolli* (softened mush). The stores contained maize, beans, amaranth, and sage, tributes paid by subjugated cities.

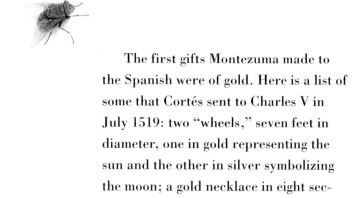

The first gifts Montezuma made to the Spanish were of gold. Here is a list of some that Cortés sent to Charles V in July 1519: two "wheels," seven feet in diameter, one in gold representing the sun and the other in silver symbolizing the moon; a gold necklace in eight sections encrusted with 183 little emeralds and 232 garnets, from which hung 27 little gold bells; a wooden helmet covered in gold; a gold mirror garnished with

GOLD IS THE SWEAT OF THE GODS

Aztec jewelry included bracelets and anklets, buckles, earrings, nose ornaments, necklaces, and pendants, all masterpieces of goldworking.

pearls; 24 shields in gold and mother-of-pearl decorated with feathers; five fish, two swans, and other birds, made from molten and beaten gold; two large shells and crocodiles in fine gold filigree, and so on. Montezuma had hoped with these gifts to persuade the conquistadors to leave his country. But nothing could have been better calculated to make them stay. The Aztecs did not fully understand that this metal represented a fortune to the Spanish. Cortés is supposed to have pretended that the gold was necessary to help them cure a disease, but this seems unlikely to have convinced the Aztecs, since they associated gold with sweat. Montezuma had concluded that the "Spanish gods" must eat the stuff! Gold and silver were the only metals worked by the Aztecs. They had

no need of iron to hoop wheels or shoe horses: they had neither horses nor wheeled transport. The Aztecs, great masters of goldsmithing, mixed gold and silver to create a polychrome effect. Another technique consisted of soaking gold in a bath of alum (sulfate of aluminum and potassium, which fixes dyes) to color it; they raised this technique to a fine art. None of this was lost on the conquistadors, who appropriated both objects and mines of gold and silver. For the Spanish, these new endeavors came cheap: the work force, first native Indians and then Africans, cost nothing, and the reserves seemed inexhaustible. Between 1492 and 1600, the export of precious metals from the Americas to Spain represented 90 percent of trade between the two continents. The ships were escorted to avoid pirates and to make salvage easier should there be a shipwreck or storm. If the accounts of the Casa de la Contratacion, or the Mint of Seville, which give us an idea of the trade, are to be believed, only 1,986 pounds came to Spain between 1503 and 1510; thirty years later, between 1531 and 1540, after the discovery and exploitation of the Americas, nearly three tons of gold and 17 tons of silver were brought in (these figures rose to eight and one-half tons of gold and over 60 tons of silver between 1551 and 1560). All this pillaged gold allowed Europe to mint a great deal more money.

Articles of gold and silver had emblematic values, reflecting the honors and social rank of those who wore them.

Aztecs liked playing games. They were particularly keen on two, *tlachtli* and *patolli*, the rules for which follow.

TLACHTLI

Two teams

For ruling-class adults

Equipment

Some rather heavy balls made of rubber, called *ulli*, about the size of bowling balls; a playing field called a *tlaxtli*, in the form of a double T, split in half in the middle and surrounded by walls; 2 stone rings fixed on the side walls.

Note

You'll want leather kneeguards, gloves, and chinguards to protect vulnerable parts of the body.

Goal of the game

To get the ball through the stone rings, using only the hips and knees.

Warnings

1) Don't throw the ball too hard; it could cause fatal injury.

2) After a game, it's best to follow the Aztec way and drain the blood from hematomas—you'll have plenty on your buttocks and hips.

IN MEXICO, PEOPLE PLAYED BASKETBALL WITH THEIR ELBOWS AND PARCHEESI WITH BEANS

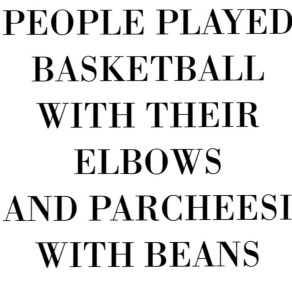

3) Don't make too many bets on the outcome, for you may lose more than just feathers, clothes, or gold—you may lose your freedom. Unless you like the idea of being a slave!

PATOLLI

Four players

A game for everyone

Equipment

Board in the form of a cross divided into 52 squares (corresponding to the number of years in an astrological cycle); beans to use as dice; small colored stones to use as counters.

Goal of the game

Players move their counters from square to square according to the number of points gained by throwing the dice. The first to get back to Start wins.

Preparation for the game

Put the board on the ground and sit around it; write a certain number of points on the beans.

Warning

This game of chance could lead you on the road to ruin and slavery. Don't bet your freedom!

The Aztecs spent a considerable amount of time interpreting omens and signs. This was how they understood the future, which was a thing that revealed, rather than created, itself. Any incident that was out of the ordinary was interpreted as the harbinger of another event, frequently disastrous. This form of speaking to the gods conditioned the Aztec way of life; they valued it more highly than human relationships. In order to know whether a certain war would end in victory, or if someone would recover from a particular disease, people would call on the astrologer, or *tonalpouhque*, who was a specialist in the sacred texts. With his help, families chose a propitious day for getting married, or baptizing a baby—whose life was already predetermined by his or her birthday. The astrologer interpreted the signs and numbers of the sacred calendar with the help of water, grains of maize, or cotton thread. This calendar was made up of "centuries" of 52-year cycles, each one containing 260 days. The Aztecs used the unit of 13 and attributed a particular significance to each number in the series. They believed implicitly in the idea of the eternal recurrence. They never tried to contradict what they had seen and faced the worst with fortitude and determination. The best example of this is how Montezuma dealt with Cortés, who he believed to be the returned god Quetzalcoatl.

If your son is born on day 7, he will be "lord, senator, rich, valiant, warriorlike; he will be courageous and brilliant in war; among those who command he will reach the gods."

If your son is born in the 13th 1 celotl, he will die a prisoner of war.

If today is day 1 coatl, merchants will find fortune on their travels.

If this man is Quetzalcoatl, the fires on the altars will be extinguished and our world will disappear forever.

If the fate of Quetzalcoatl has the sign 1 acatl in the ascendant, he will appear in the east as the morning star.

IF THIS MAN IS QUETZALCOATL . . . READING AZTEC FORTUNES

If this man is the incarnation of Quetzalcoatl, I cannot sacrifice strangers to Huitzilopochtli. It would be criminal; I would not have respected the gods.

If the earth has trembled several times, this man is Quetzalcoatl.

If this being accepts food from flesh and blood, this means he recognizes the country as his own and that he is a god.

If I hear the owl hoot, or if a rabbit comes into a house, if a wolf crosses my path, then misfortune is close.

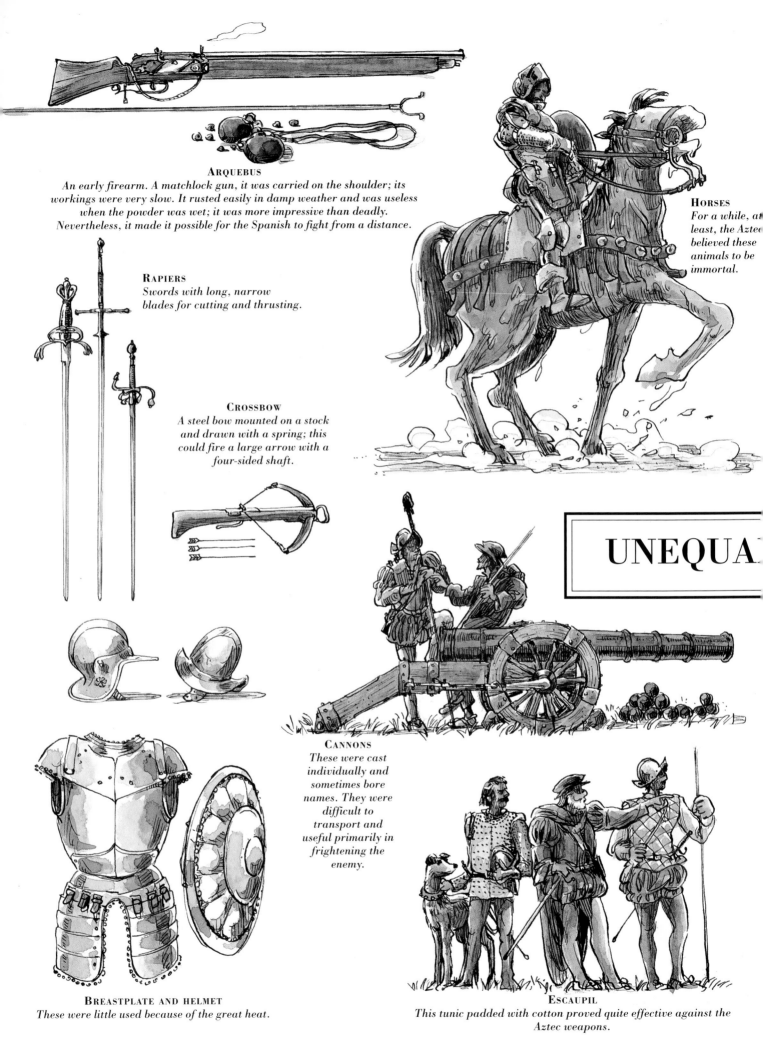

ARQUEBUS
An early firearm. A matchlock gun, it was carried on the shoulder; its workings were very slow. It rusted easily in damp weather and was useless when the powder was wet; it was more impressive than deadly. Nevertheless, it made it possible for the Spanish to fight from a distance.

HORSES
For a while, at least, the Aztec believed these animals to be immortal.

RAPIERS
Swords with long, narrow blades for cutting and thrusting.

CROSSBOW
A steel bow mounted on a stock and drawn with a spring; this could fire a large arrow with a four-sided shaft.

UNEQUA

CANNONS
These were cast individually and sometimes bore names. They were difficult to transport and useful primarily in frightening the enemy.

BREASTPLATE AND HELMET
These were little used because of the great heat.

ESCAUPIL
This tunic padded with cotton proved quite effective against the Aztec weapons.

FEATHERED SHIELD

Aztec warriors carried round shields made of jaguar skin stretched over a wood frame, about 20 to 30 inches in diameter, and decorated with feathers, often the red and yellow feathers of parrots.

FEATHER HEADDRESS

Cuauhtémoc, the last Aztec emperor, wore one of these. He believed that his headdress, which had been left him by his father, had magic powers—it would make the enemy turn and flee at the mere sight of it.

Javelin or lance, long and thin, made of wood with an obsidian point; usually propelled with an atlatl spear-thrower.

Being a warrior was an honor. Boys began learning the arts of war at age 15.

FLINT KNIVES

Highly sharp knives made of flint have been found in the Great Temple, and such knives were also used in war.

IN ARMS

MASKS

Made of feathers set in a frame, these masks, like European heraldry, served to distinguish among the Aztec warriors. The Aztecs also thought the masks gave warriors magical powers. They used war cries to frighten their opponents. In actual fact, these only gave away the Aztecs' positions to the Spanish.

WARRIOR COSTUMES

Aztec warriors wore elaborate costumes. The more prisoners a warrior had taken, the more complicated his costume became.

PADDED COTTON ARMOR

The ichcahuipilli ("cotton bodice") was so effective that the Spaniards wore them in preference to their steel armor, which was heavy and hot.

SPEAR AND TWO-HANDED SWORD

Made of hardwood; the swords were about 1 yard long and were set with obsidian blades. Obsidian is a green or black mineral with a shimmering appearance. It can be made into razor-sharp blades (the Aztec swords could cut off a horse's head in one blow). Because of its glassy properties, it was also used to make mirrors.

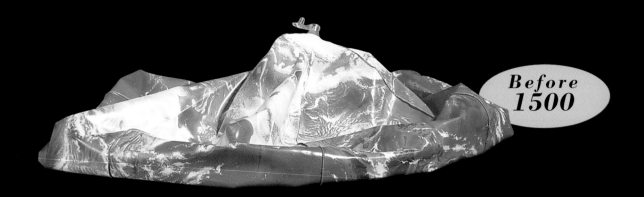

Before
1500

UNFORTUNATELY FOR THE AZTECS, AT THE BEGINNING OF THE FIFTEENTH CENTURY, THE WORLD BECAME ROUND

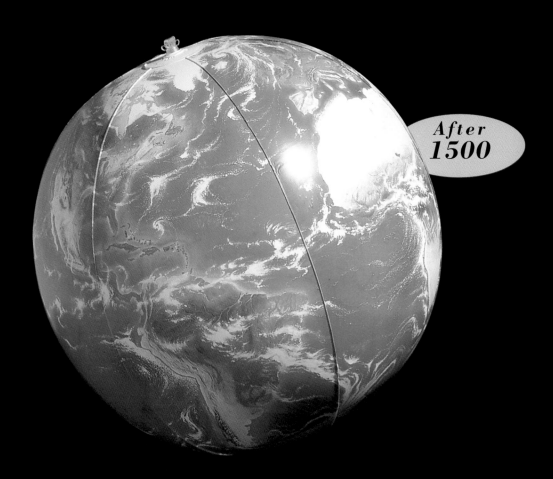

After
1500

According to medieval geography, our world consisted of 85 percent land and 15 percent water. A famous Catalan atlas of 1375 placed Jerusalem at the center of the world. In fact, the idea we have of our planet depends very largely on our modern technical know-how; in the fifteenth century, a sailor was completely without points of reference once he was out of sight of the shore. Somewhat like a child who gradually becomes braver in the dark, men dared to extend the area of their discoveries. They moved from practical navigation to something more scientific, using the astrolabe and compasses to journey by the stars.

The great European dream from Marco Polo (1254-1323) onward had been to reach India without being at the mercy of the Arabs. The Mediterranean Sea had been extensively explored—the Atlantic Ocean remained a mystery. The adventure began in 1415 when the Portuguese, led by Henry the Navigator, won the battle of Ceuta. This town in northern Morocco had become the lair of Barbary pirates who struck terror into the Mediterranean. Little by little, the Portuguese advanced: Madeira (1418), the Azores, (1431), the Canaries (1434), the Cape Verde Islands (1437). As they moved from headland to headland, Africa took shape: Cape Bajador in 1434, Cape Blanc in 1441, Cape Verde in 1445, Cape Palmas in 1460. They crossed the African equator in 1475. With great care, they systematically calculated all the latitudes, with the aid of their astrolabes. In 1482, King John II asked the navigator Diogo Cão to find a sea route linking Europe to Asia via Africa. Cão explored the coast of southwest Africa. Bartolomeu Dias followed in his wake and rounded the bottom tip of the continent, the Cape of Good Hope, in 1488. In the hope of traveling farther eastward, John II deliberately chose to ignore Christopher Columbus' plans, despite the fact that the latter had been living in Portugal for many years and was married to a high-ranking Portuguese lady. Columbus hoped to reach the Indies—but by going west! In 1498 Vasco da Gama reached India by sea. The race was on: from east to west, the earth was growing larger and rounder.

But it was not until 1519-22 that Magellan made the first round-the-world voyage. And only a few years later, Nicholas Copernicus (1473-1543) started to question the idea that the earth was the center of the universe.

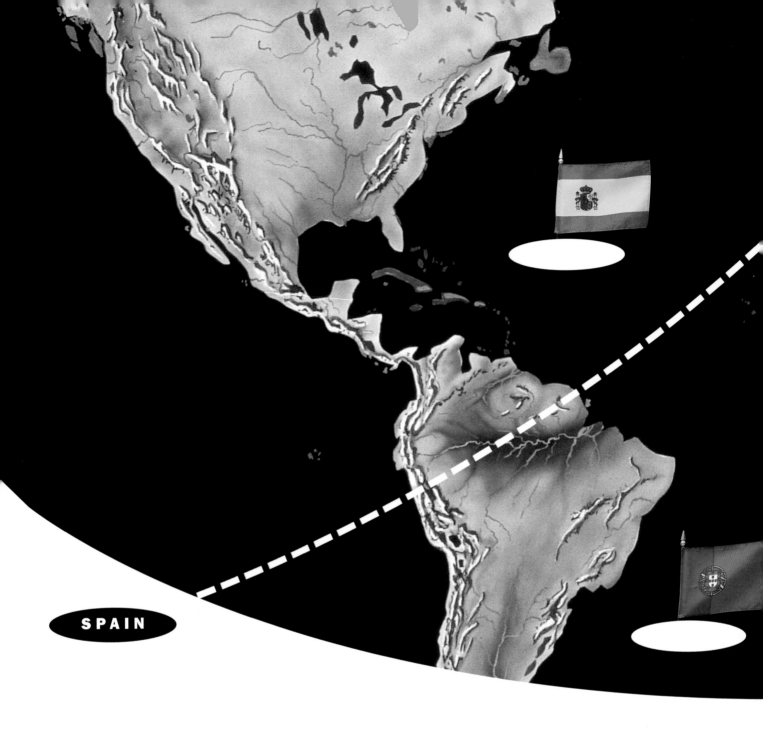

SPAIN

WITH THE TREATY OF
TORDESILLAS,
THE POPE DIVIDES THE WORLD

PORTUGAL

"To Ferdinand and Isabella, by the grace of God, king and queen of Castile, Leon, Aragon, Sicily, Grenada, Toledo, Valencia, Galicia . . . His Highness, the king of Portugal, our dearly beloved brother, has sent us his ambassadors and dignitaries . . . in order to establish, to confirm, and to come to an agreement with us . . . over to whom the oceans remaining to be discovered should belong." Thus begins the Treaty of Tordesillas, a symbol of the rivalry between Spain and Portugal in the conquest of the world. The Portuguese were the first to send out explorations in the fifteenth century, but after Columbus discovered the Americas for Spain, these two nations vied with each other for world dominance. It was 1494 and the Portuguese were demanding recognition of a demarcation line agreed a year earlier. Brokered by

Pope Alexander VI, a Spaniard, this treaty was signed on June 7 by both sovereigns. The world was divided in two according to a meridian 370 leagues from the westernmost island of the Cape Verde archipelago. Portugal retained the sea route to India and got Brazil, while the rest of South and Central America became Spanish. France and England reacted several years later, but with great force. "I would like to see the clause in Adam's testament that excludes me from sharing the world," Francis I is supposed to have said. The Treaty of Tordesillas is therefore at the root of many conflicts between the European powers on the Atlantic coast. But what was the price the pope was asking for his good offices? That the peoples of the new continents be converted to Christianity.

The "New" World that Christopher Columbus discovered in 1492 was quite old to the Aztecs: to the peoples of the American continents it was the Europeans who were the newcomers. The most important moment of this encounter between two very different worlds was when Montezuma met Cortés: the leader of one empire was meeting an emissary from another. Cortés was serving Spain, which was then ruled by the Holy Roman emperor Charles V—who didn't even visit Spain until he was 17. In fact, Charles inherited a truly vast empire, and his full title, more or less, was "Charles, king of the Romans, elected Emperor, forever Augustus, king of Spain, king of Naples, Jerusalem, the Balearic Isles, and the Indian and Canary islands, king of the continent across the ocean, archduke of Austria, duke of Brabant, Burgundy, Styria, Carinthia, Tyrol, Luxembourg, Limburg, Athens . . . count of Hapsburg and Flanders . . . prince palatinate of Burgundy and Hainault . . . landgrave of Germany . . . lord in Africa and Asia." And so on. In the same way that the pope was supposed to be the servant of God on earth in spiritual matters, the Holy Roman emperor was supposed to be God's temporal servant. The emperor claimed to be the supreme ruler of all Christendom. He wasn't, of course. Outside the empire, the emperor was sometimes given authority, sometimes not. Like the other rulers of Europe during that time, Charles V was heavily involved in religious matters: "protecting the faith" meant dealing with the growing Protestant Reformation, and it also meant deciding what to do with non-Christians, meaning Jews and Moslems. In Spain, in particular, protecting the faith had a sad story. A decree of 1412 forbade Jewish people from holding public office, forced them to live in ghettos, and made them wear a red circle on their clothing. Even worse, in 1492, they were forced to choose between being baptized Christians or leaving the country—those who stayed behind and were not baptized were to be executed. Not surprisingly, 150,000 opted for conversion, but 150,000 to 200,000 chose exile in Portugal, North Africa, or the eastern Mediterranean. Ironically, the day set for their

departure was also the date on which Columbus set sail: as he set off on his voyage west, thousands of other people were being thrown out of their homes. The same cruel policy was applied to Moslems, who were being punished for not being Christian and for eight centuries of conquest in Spain and Portugal (711-1492). They were put under such severe pressure that at the end of the sixteenth century they revolted. In addition to such persecutions, there was also the Inquisition. In 1478, King Ferdinand and Queen Isabella of Spain managed to get approval from Pope Sixtus IV to establish the Spanish Inquisition. In 1483, the government chose Tomás de Torquemada to be the first inquisitor general; in fact, he was largely responsible for the expulsion of the Jews in 1492. Torquemada's goal was to root out all forms of heresy. He saw it as his duty to create a nation that was spiritually and ideologically homogeneous to better serve the monarchy. The popes tried to curb the cruel excesses of the Spanish Inquisition, but over the years it had become a useful tool of the increasingly powerful monarchy.

CHARLES V, KEEPING THE FAITH

WHO HAD
A TASTE
FOR
CONQUISTADORS?

"Human flesh cooked with maize," from the codex of Bernardino de Sahagún, sixteenth century.

The men who set off for the Americas were drawn for the most part from the minor nobility, the hidalgos. Some of them had aristocratic educations, many of them were short of money. What were they like? They were eager for adventure, they were eager for riches, they were willing to embark on any adventure. In the Americas they saw the opportunity to achieve what they could not achieve in Spain: to become important, to be admired for wealth and accomplishments, both as a Christian and as a knight. *Ir a valer mas* ("to set forth to be worth more") was the conquistador's motto.

THE QUEST FOR ADVENTURE

Many future conquistadors got their taste for adventure from reading. Printing with movable type had just been invented in Europe, and tales of the exciting exploits of knights were popular. These usually told the story of a hero of noble birth; his past is vague, perhaps troubled, but he achieves brilliant victories in faraway lands, on distant and exotic seas and islands. Blessed with endless courage and a stout heart, these heroes personified the self-confidence that Spain felt at that time. The conquistadors likened themselves to the greatest of the ancients. Bernal Díaz del Castillo, proud of his prowess, states that he "has taken part in more battles than Julius Caesar." The power of these stories on the imagination was even greater because the authors claimed that they drew their stories from historical facts.

RELIGIOUS FAITH

Many conquistadors believed they had a divine mission (or that was the excuse they gave); they claimed to burn with the passion to combat the adversaries of Christ, to convert the heathen Indians, to teach them the true faith. This "duty" was supported by the *requerimento*, made law in Burgos in 1513: each expedition had to include a notary, who was to obtain from the natives their recognition of the authority of the king of Castile and of the pope and their acceptance of the Catholic faith (much like the demands the Aztecs themselves made on neighboring towns). Then, as soon as the pagan idols had been destroyed and replaced by a statue of the Virgin Mary, the chaplain would baptize them.

THE LUST FOR GOLD

Far and away the greatest motivation was the lust for gold. The conquistadors hoped to get rich, quickly and easily. They dreamed of sudden fortunes. They were all the more strongly motivated because agriculture, industry, and commerce were in crisis in Spain: a series of poor harvests was causing high infant mortality, rising prices, a fall in exports, and a general shrinking of the markets. To find gold a man had to be lucky, but it was easier to be lucky overseas, and finding gold meant finding the means to make one's fortune.

CHRISTOPHER COLUMBUS
(1451-1506)
He made four great voyages of discovery between 1492 to 1504. He discovered the Caribbean islands, but believed he was somewhere in Asia, which is why to this day native Americans are called Indians.

JOHN CABOT
(c. 1451-c. 1498)
He crossed the Atlantic for the English king Henry VII and explored the North American coast, including Newfoundland, in 1497-98.

GIOVANNI DA VERRAZANO
(1485-1528)
A Florentine in the service of Francis I, he sailed along the North American coast from North Carolina to Newfoundland and was probably the first European to enter New York Bay.

WHO WON THE FIRST TRANS-ATLANTIC RACE IN HISTORY ?

The story of discovery is really the story of a succession of discoveries, none of which would have been possible without the one before. Everything began when Christopher Columbus, son of a Genoese weaver and resident in Portugal since 1476, decided to reach Asia by the Atlantic route, which he assumed to be very short. He submitted his plan to King John II of Portugal and to the kings and queens of England, France, and Spain. It was finally the rulers of Spain who gave him the title of admiral and entrusted him with a fleet of three caravels. Columbus's voyage was to lead to a collision between two worlds, that of the peoples of Europe and that of the peoples of the American continents. Because of Columbus, Montezuma would someday meet Cortés, and after that meeting both worlds would never be the same.

FERDINAND MAGELLAN
(c. 1480-1521)
This Portuguese navigator discovered the straits that bear his name in 1520 during the first circumnavigation of the world (1519-22).

PEDRO ALVARES CABRAL
(1460-1526)
This Portuguese navigator discovered Brazil in 1500.

JACQUES CARTIER
(1491-1557)
French navigator sent by Francis I to explore the eastern shore of America; he reached Newfoundland and other areas of Canada, which he claimed for the French throne (1534-36).

HERNÁN CORTÉS, JUST ANOTHER HIDALGO

Cortés' parents belonged to minor nobility in the Estremadura region of central Spain. His father had only modest means and thought that his son should enter the army or become a magistrate. In 1499, seven years after Columbus arrived in the Americas, Hernán was sent to the university of Salamanca. He was 14 years old.

Most of Europe was then involved in the Italian Wars, but Hernán decided not to seek glory in combat and instead idled away his time in port cities, such as Seville and Cadiz. By this time Christopher Columbus was involved in his last trips back and forth between Spain and the Caribbean. The port of Seville had become the central area for imports and exports, although Tinto, Palos, and Málaga were also active between 1492 and 1500. Seville was far from ideal because it was small; boats that reached below a certain depth in the water had to take on part of their cargo in Cadiz, while passengers had to embark at Sanlúcar de Barrameda. Maintenance services for large ships were also inadequate. Even so, Seville became the administrative center of Spain's maritime traffic and headquarters of the navigation school founded by the Italian navigator Amerigo Vespucci, in whose honor America was named. Because of their many expeditions to the east, the Portuguese had a more highly developed maritime organization, with about twenty working ports. Cortés was 19 years old when he embarked on a merchant ship in the port of Sanlúcar that was bound for Santo Domingo, on the island of Haiti. His father had given him his blessing and a little money. It was 1504, and Cortés was beginning his career as a conquistador by serving as a public scribe.

Did the 19-year-old Hernán Cortés think that someday his picture would appear on the money of his homeland?

HOW THE SPANISH DISCOVERED MEXICO AT A SNAIL'S PACE

Since 1492, the center of interest for many fortune-hunters had been the Antilles and other Caribbean islands. Christopher Columbus had taken 69 days to cross the Atlantic. His son, Diego, who had been governor and viceroy of the West Indies since 1504, decided to begin the systematic exploration of Cuba, and that island soon became a natural stepping-stone between the Old and

Cuba is just 500 miles from the Yucatan coast, but it took the Spanish 25 years to cover the distance.

New Worlds. He entrusted the expedition to the conquistador Diego de Velázquez, who then declared himself governor of the island. His secretary and treasurer was none other than the 26-year-old Hernán Cortés. By then, the Spanish had reached the southeast coast of Cuba, only 500 miles from the Yucatan peninsula. Between 1517 and 1519 the first reconnaissance expeditions to the Yucatan were carried out under the command of Fernández de Córdoba and Juan de Grijalva. The Gulf of Mexico was beginning to become known, but these journeys exacted a high price in terms of shipwrecks and bloody confrontations with the natives. Some peaceful contacts were made, and friendly local chiefs gave them gold and gifts. The Spanish then started to ask themselves: what had all those men died for? Well, a new land had been discovered. And now it was ripe for exploration.

America is more than 9,000 miles from Europe, but Christopher Columbus made the journey in just 69 days.

CAPTAIN CORTÉS AND HIS CREW ARE HAPPY TO WELCOME YOU ABOARD

In 1511, Cortés took part in the conquest of Cuba with Diego de Velázquez and became actively involved in the administration of the new colony. In the winter of 1518-19, Cortés and his men left Santiago on orders from the governor to search the island for provisions, soldiers, and adventurers. In Trinidad Square, you would have heard this public announcement three times a day: "Listen up! In the name of the king! Know that the fleet anchored at Trinidad is sailing to the west with the authorization of the governor. Lively business, solid houses, land to be discovered await those who wish to accompany Captain Cortés. Enroll under his flag in the name of God and the king!" Bernal Díaz del Castillo tells us, "As news of the expedition spread through the island and Cortés wrote to his friends urging them to prepare to undertake this voyage with him, many sold their land to buy arms and horses, others started to prepare cassava [flour made from the root of dried manioc] and salt pork." This expedition, like many others in the previous hundred years, was based not on a contract between colleagues but on custom and law. Sometimes individuals shared the profits and losses of an expedition in proportion to the amount of money or work they had invested, while those who worked for them received a salary. But in this case, one-fifth of the booty was to go to the king; the next claimants were the leader and his officers; then the soldiers; and lastly those who had invested money, arms, horses, and ships. Who was the leader? It was the captain, and the captain was Cortés. He organized the expedition, made the decisions, and supervised everything that was undertaken. He was much loved by his sailors and men, from whom he demanded absolute obedience and courage. He looked for people able to deal with a hostile natural environment and not afraid to battle the fiercest attacks. In February 1519, Cortés slipped out of port under cover (because Velázquez had changed his mind); after a last stopover in Havana, they set sail on the open sea. The fleet consisted of 11 ships, 553 soldiers (including 32 men armed with crossbows and 13 with arquebuses), 110 sailors, 16 horses, and 14 cannons. Also on board were a notary to claim possession of the new lands for the king; the friars Juan Dias and Bartolomé de Olmedo to assure the natives' conversion to Christianity; an astrologer named Botello; two native interpreters, called Melchor and Julian; Orthiz, a lute and violin player; several women for domestic work; and among the officers Pedro de Alvarado, future conqueror of Guatemala and Salvador, and Francisco de Montejo, future governor of Honduras and the Yucatan.

HOW CORTÉS TORE UP HIS RETURN TICKET

Velázquez, governor of Cuba, ordered Cortés to locate suitable areas for settlement on the Mexican coast, to found colonies there, and then to join the expeditions led by Grijalva and Niescuesa. Cortés set off from Santiago de Cuba with six ships but had eleven when he arrived on the Mexican coast. First, Cortés was made admiral of the fleet with the authority of Velázquez, "by the grace of God, for the furtherance of our faith, and in the service of His Majesty"; but when he slipped out of Santiago with his men and arms he had the arms of Castile embroidered on his flag. In so doing, he proclaimed his loyalty to the crown of Spain; "He was accused of already being in revolt by leaving port under cover; it was claimed he had boasted that he would be captain, whatever Velázquez thought about it, and that for this reason he had boarded his men by night, so that if he was stripped of office, he could set sail anyway." When he arrived in the Yucatan, Cortés founded the town of Villa Rica de la Vera Cruz, and threw off any remaining allegiance to Velázquez. More

than once, his behavior jeopardized the success of his enterprise (his journey was to take him from Santiago de Cuba to Trinidad, Havana, the island of Cozumel, the northeast of Yucatan, the Mexican peninsula, and finally Tabasco and San Juan de Ulua). On several occasions, Velázquez sent letters and orders to Cortés, trying to force him to reduce his operations. He considered Cortés a rebel. And on several occasions, the conquistador "wrote to Velázquez in very ingratiating terms, with many promises—he was very good at that—saying that he would leave the following day, and serve Velázquez." However, Cortés wanted to pursue the expedition on his own terms and felt he was under the authority of no one but the emperor Charles V. To escape Velázquez' threats, he found a legal loophole. When he built the town of Villa Rica de la Vera Cruz, he handed over all the administrative apparatus of which he was officially in charge to its appointed mayor. Then he had himself called before the mayor, who chose him as captain general and declared invalid the duties he had carried out under Velázquez. Thus Cortés gave up his official duties and had himself appointed commander-in-chief of a new colony, serving in the name of the king of Spain (Charles V), to whom he sent a report in which he asked to have his nomination ratified. With the report he sent along a gift of some gold to bear witness to his achievement. Some of the conquistadors with Cortés were still loyal to Velázquez and wanted to return to Cuba. Rather than risk losing the men and the part of his fleet they would take with them, Cortés had all of his boats sunk except one. In that way he brought a final end to his relations with the Spaniards in Cuba. He and his men were on their own.

TRANSLATIOI

Cortés at Montezuma's court. Doña Marina stands to the right of Cortés. Painting by Juan Ortega (1885).

When Cortés set off inland, he expected to meet tribes of natives like those the Spanish had encountered elsewhere: he had no idea he was about to make contact with an empire. One of his major concerns was speaking with the natives. He had left Cuba with two native interpreters, called Melchor and Julian by the Spanish, but they proved inadequate and were soon replaced by two new acquaintances: Geronimo de Aguilar and an Aztec girl the Spanish named Doña Marina, who became Cortés' mistress and closest adviser. Aguilar had been shipwrecked off the Mexican coast in 1511. All of his shipmates had perished except for Gonzalo Guerrero, with whom he had been washed up on the Yucatan peninsula. Guerrero had quickly learned the language of the country and been singled out by

BY DOÑA MARINA

a native chief who gave him military duties. He had adopted the native customs and religion and had married a woman of high birth. He painted his body, let his hair grow long, and pierced his ears. When the conquistadors arrived, he fled. Aguilar, however, had been enslaved and was eager to join the Spanish as an interpreter, translating the Mayan language. The Aztec girl came as a gift. As Cortés explored the country and claimed it in the name of Spain, he occasionally fought battles with the natives, but a few cannon shots were usually enough to drive off attacks. Some tribes sought to make peace with the Spanish and gave them gifts, including women. This is how Doña Marina came to join the Spanish. Her native tongue was Nahuatl, the language of the Aztecs, but she also knew local dialects and soon learned Spanish. She was important to Cortés in other ways, for she told Cortés of the weaknesses of the Aztec Empire, in particular the fact that the subject tribes in the provinces hated the Aztecs and were eager to rebel against them. She also told him that the Aztecs were expecting the return of the exiled god Quetzalcoatl and that he was being mistaken for that god. This information would soon prove invaluable. Cortés was never without his two interpreters, and every word was carefully translated for him. He himself never learned Nahuatl, although it was later declared an official language by the Spanish. (The priests who soon arrived in the New World were the first Europeans to learn it—they used it in order to force Christianity on the natives.) Even with his interpreters, Cortés encountered great problems: the linguistic diversity of the Aztec Empire made communication extremely difficult. Sometimes two or three languages were spoken in the same town. When Cortés first met Montezuma, they conversed politely with the aid of Doña Marina. Cortés later had a son with Marina, perhaps the first of the mestizos (mixed-bloods).

THE ROUTE
OF CONQUEST

In April 1519, Cortés and his men explored the Yucatan coast and visited Indian villages, such as San Juan de Ulua. The Spanish were immediately received by Tendile, an Aztec governor, who showered them with gifts of gold. He had been entrusted by Montezuma with the mission of preventing the Spanish troops from advancing deeper into Aztec territory.

During the summer of 1519, the town of Villa Rica de la Vera Cruz was founded. Cortés rejected Velázquez' authority and marched toward Cempoalla, the Totonac capital. This tribe had only recently been conquered by the Aztecs and quickly sided with the Spanish, who thereby gained 400 soldiers.

The road between Cempoalla and Jalapa crossed thick jungle. In their heavy, padded armor, the Spanish suffered dreadfully from the heat and humidity. They climbed a mountain range and skirted the flanks of the mountain Nauchampatepetl before crossing an endless succession of mountain valleys.

They arrived at Tlaxcala in September 1519. This town lies at 7,500 feet and is built on four hills linked by strong bastion walls. The Spanish attacked, but when the Tlaxcalans realized the Spanish were not allies of the Aztecs, they signed an agreement with the Spanish. Cortés now had even more soldiers in his army.

In October 1519, they reached the sacred Aztec city of Cholula. Suspicious of the warm welcome they were given, the Spanish discovered poorly concealed trenches and wooden defenses and decided that the city's nobility had been planning an ambush. With the aid of the Tlaxcalans, the conquistadors easily won the ensuing battle, which became a slaughter.

In the days that followed, Cortés and ten of his men climbed one of the two active volcanoes in the Valley of Mexico; this was Popocatépetl, which is 17,887 feet high. Fighting the cold and heat, they managed this climb clad in sandals with their capes wrapped tightly round them—the ascent was not repeated by Europeans until 1827.

On November 1, Cortés continued his march on Tenochtitlán. Only 62 miles remained; behind him lay 185 miles leading back to Cempoalla. On November 7, on the south side of Lake Texcoco, he negotiated with Montezuma's ambassadors, who repeated their advice not to pursue his journey . . . Within hours he was standing before the emperor.

The route followed by Cortés during the conquest of Mexico on a sixteenth-century map. National Museum of Mexico.

So here he is, finally, this man covered in gold, emeralds, and fancy feathers. How old is he? Forty? Or maybe fifty-two, as the natives claim. If that's true, his dark skin, slim figure, and short hair make him look younger. I've waited six months to meet him, and here he is, with slaves who sweep the ground he walks on and crowds of princes and priests following him around everywhere.

Montezuma respects me for my bravery, but even more he believes we're gods. Should we go along with this fancy ceremony or should we be suspicious and prepare to fight? My official duty is to convert him to Catholicism, get him to abdicate in favor of my king, and take possession of his wealth. There's gold everywhere here, and I'll bet there's a lot more hidden away. My men and I are ready to fight to the death.

The two men exchanged gifts as symbols of their mutual recognition: Cortés gave Montezuma a necklace of pearls and cut glass perfumed with musk, and Montezuma gave Cortés two necklaces of shells each hung with eight large shrimp made of fine gold. The kings of Texcoco and Tacuba came forward, exchanged a few words of greeting with Cortés, and paid homage to him. Then Aztec officials led the group of Spaniards off to large apartments that had been prepared for them.

The meeting of Montezuma and Cortés by an anonymous artist.

MONTEZUMA AND CORTÉS: WHAT WERE THEY THINKING?

Montezuma & Cortés in the City of Mexico

Drakes Voyages

The first meeting of Montezuma and Cortés took place outside the gates of Tenochtitlán on November 8, 1519. Let's imagine what each of them, with all his prejudices, fears, and hopes, might have been thinking.

I am indeed in the presence of a man who commands the thunder and the animal world. This *teule* [demigod] has shown us his power. Is he perhaps Quetzalcoatl, the god who went east and who promised us he would return to reclaim his kingdom? If so I, Montezuma II, may hold my people's destiny in my hands; if Quetzalcoatl wants his possessions back, I must respect the will of the gods. But I do not understand this divine message! Tomorrow, like today and yesterday, I shall sacrifice young children to Huitzilopochtli, god of war. He is my only help; perhaps inspiration will come to me! Moreover, I must not delay in calling my court to council to decide how we may best rid ourselves of these evil and unexpected visitors. I have offered them gold to persuade them to leave our land. Why are they still here? I do not understand, and sometimes these uncertainties paralyze me.

THE MOST ASTONISHING HOSTAGE-TAKING IN HISTORY

Montezuma received Cortés and his men in the palace built by his father, the emperor Axayacatl. As had become his habit, he took the Spaniard by the hand and led him through his richly decorated apartments. They dined together, and Cortés told the emperor of his faith and tried, without success, to convert Montezuma to Christianity. Montezuma was polite and expressed his admiration. Both men continued to treat each other with respect and courtesy. On the fourth day, the conquistadors were taken on their first tour of the city. First they went to the main marketplace and saw the hundreds of merchants and the variety of goods on sale. Then they went through the gardens and streets that led to the temple, the temple from whose summit one could see allied towns; the temple where sacrifice took place. And lastly, they were shown the sumptuous treasure of Axayacatl.

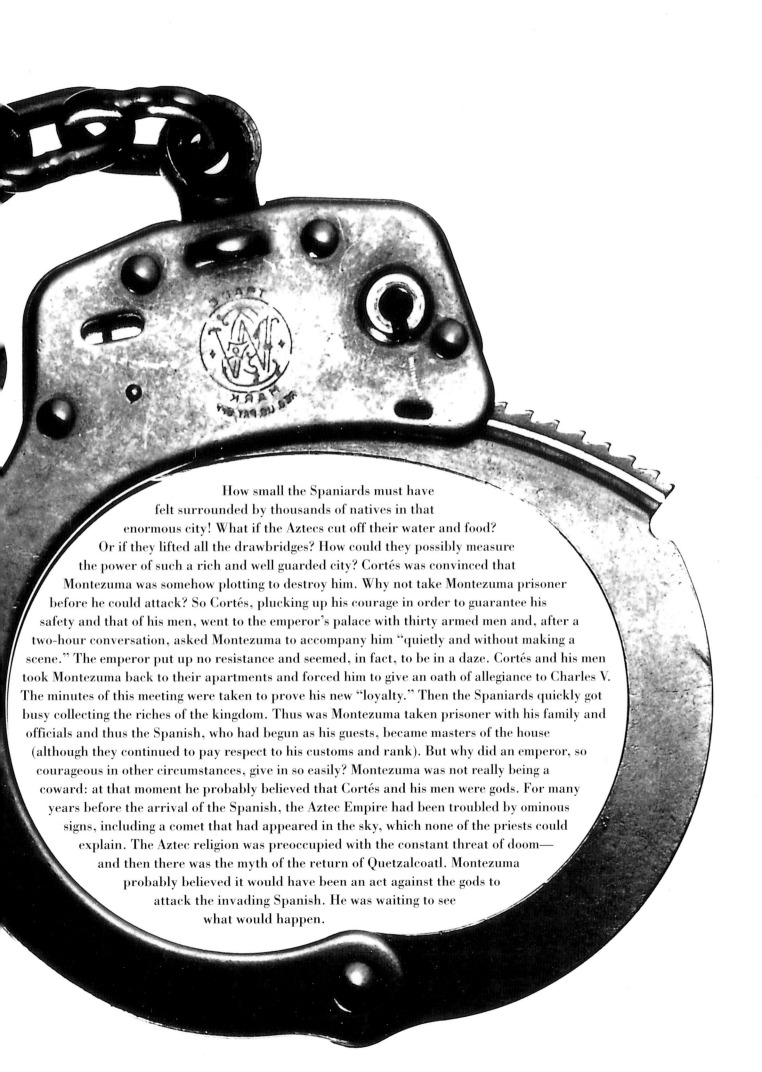

How small the Spaniards must have
felt surrounded by thousands of natives in that
enormous city! What if the Aztecs cut off their water and food?
Or if they lifted all the drawbridges? How could they possibly measure
the power of such a rich and well guarded city? Cortés was convinced that
Montezuma was somehow plotting to destroy him. Why not take Montezuma prisoner
before he could attack? So Cortés, plucking up his courage in order to guarantee his
safety and that of his men, went to the emperor's palace with thirty armed men and, after a
two-hour conversation, asked Montezuma to accompany him "quietly and without making a
scene." The emperor put up no resistance and seemed, in fact, to be in a daze. Cortés and his men
took Montezuma back to their apartments and forced him to give an oath of allegiance to Charles V.
The minutes of this meeting were taken to prove his new "loyalty." Then the Spaniards quickly got
busy collecting the riches of the kingdom. Thus was Montezuma taken prisoner with his family and
officials and thus the Spanish, who had begun as his guests, became masters of the house
(although they continued to pay respect to his customs and rank). But why did an emperor, so
courageous in other circumstances, give in so easily? Montezuma was not really being a
coward: at that moment he probably believed that Cortés and his men were gods. For many
years before the arrival of the Spanish, the Aztec Empire had been troubled by ominous
signs, including a comet that had appeared in the sky, which none of the priests could
explain. The Aztec religion was preoccupied with the constant threat of doom—
and then there was the myth of the return of Quetzalcoatl. Montezuma
probably believed it would have been an act against the gods to
attack the invading Spanish. He was waiting to see
what would happen.

MONTEZ MURDER OR SUICI

UMA:

DE ?

Having allowed himself to be taken prisoner by the conquistadors without a struggle in his own home, Montezuma rapidly lost his authority in the eyes of his people. When the first skirmishes of the Noche Triste, or "Sad Night," began, the Spanish urged the emperor to use his influence to dampen the ferocity of the warriors and stop the fighting. After some hesitation, "Montezuma said, 'I am convinced that I will certainly not be able to persuade them to stop the war, because they have chosen another emperor and have sworn not to leave any one of you alive. I believe you will die in this city.' Even so, at the height of one of the biggest attacks, Montezuma decided to go out on the balcony of one of the terraces, protected by a large number of our men . . . But the men noticed that the firing stopped while Montezuma was speaking, and so they took less care to protect him. It was then that the unfortunate king was struck by three stones and arrows in the head, arm, and leg. We begged him to let himself be taken care of, and to eat something, but, despite all the comforting words we could give him, he would do nothing; suddenly, although we least expected it, we learned that he was dead. Cortés wept for him as did all our captains and soldiers . . . When they heard he was dead, the Aztecs sent up great wailings and sad cries that reached as far as us. But their attacks got no less fierce."

So runs the Spanish version: Montezuma had been hit by one of his own people and refused all aid. He would not allow himself to be baptized, but he entrusted his sons to Cortés. His body was given to the Aztecs, who burned it according to Aztec tradition. The emperor had died before witnessing the destruction and extermination of his city and his people. His worst fears would soon be realized.

On June 30, 1520, nearly eight months after the meeting of Montezuma and Cortés, the Spaniards fled Tenochtitlán, running for their lives and leaving behind much of the stolen Aztec treasure. This was the *Noche Triste* ("sad night"). How had it come about?

On May 4, Cortés had left the capital to go and meet what he believed to be reinforcements from Spain. He had left one of his trusted men, Pedro de Alvarado, in command of the Spanish garrison and had given the Aztecs permission to celebrate the great annual feast of Toxcatl in his absence on condition that no human sacrifice occur. He had then set off, but found no reinforcements on the coast. Instead, the fleet anchored at San Juan de Ulua came from Cuba and was led by Pánfilo de Narváez, who had been sent by Velázquez to find Cortés and make him pay for his "treachery." As soon as Cortés had left Cuba for Mexico, the governor "started commissioning, with great thoroughness, any boat on the island that could be used; he brought together soldiers and captains to send off a great fleet to arrest Cortés and ourselves. He was so keen to get ready that he went himself from town to town, hamlet to hamlet, writing to his friends in all the parts of the island he could not go to himself, asking them to help him in this expedition. Within eleven or twelve months, he had got eighteen ships of

N THE SAD NIGHT

varying sizes and about 1,300 soldiers, including captains and sailors." Cortés and some of his men met Narváez at Cempoalla; following a short battle, they took Narváez prisoner and then returned to Tenochtitlán, reinforced by those of Narváez's troops who had defected to his side. By the time they returned, on June 24, serious trouble had broken out. Alvarado had taken advantage of the Aztec celebration to slaughter nearly a thousand of the highest Aztec nobles while they were unarmed and engaged in a ritual dance. Not surprisingly, the Aztecs were enraged, and their reprisals were swift and ruthless. Aztec warriors came from all corners of the Valley of Mexico. A Spanish witness tells us, "Neither cannons nor arquebuses, nor crossbows, nor the vigor with which we fought in the melee, nor the thirty or forty men we killed with each attack, nothing could stop them; they regrouped, kept

their formation and fell upon us with even greater fury. When we appeared to gain a little ground or part of a street, it was because they fell back on purpose to draw us on and ever further away from our lodgings, so that we would be easier targets: they hoped that no Spaniard would return alive to barracks." This was a crucial period for the besieged Spanish, who were forced to eat their horses to survive. On June 25, the revolt became an all-out rebellion; not even Cortés with his reinforcements could achieve anything. On the night of June 30, a night of pouring rain, Cortés and his men fled the city, chased by the Aztecs, who fought them all the way: this was the Noche Triste, for by dawn of the next day, two-thirds of the Spanish and almost all their native allies had been killed, and they had lost all their artillery. The fighting ended only when they reached the safety of Tlaxcala.

AFTER THREE MONTHS OF SIEGE,
FAT RATS LOOK TASTY

For over a year after the Noche Triste, Cortés prepared to return to Tenochtitlán. He concentrated his time and attention on two things: getting the towns that bordered Lake Texcoco under his sway and building a fleet that would carry him into the heart of the city. He understood that the lakes and lagoons had to be under his control if he was to conquer the city. He was assisted in this strategic planning by his master shipbuilder, Martín Lopez.

Engraving showing the siege of Tenochtitlán.

The final fleet consisted of thirteen small two-masted sailing ships, each with a bridge and cannon, and 1,600 boats powered by oars, all of them designed to cross the shallow waters of the Lake Texcoco. These ships were taken apart into pieces, with each piece numbered so that the ships could be quickly assembled at the lake, and then transported across the more than 60 miles to the lake by 8,000 slaves. The larger pieces were rolled forward on logs. To make launching the ships easier, a canal over a mile long and 12 feet wide was dug. A detailed map of the lagoon was drawn up to help navigate. Finally, despite the difficulties Cortés had finding rowers—his Spanish hidalgos considered the work too demeaning—the fleet set sail for Tenochtitlán under Cortés' command on May 20, 1521. The siege of the city had begun.

On land, the army was divided into three companies to attack the three causeways linking Tenochtitlán to the mainland. Each company was led by a lieutenant and was composed of tens of thousands of Tlaxcalans, Otomi, Chalca, and Xochimilco warriors: Alvarado took Tlacopán, Olid Coyoacan, and Sandoval besieged Tepeyac, all with the order to leave the causeway open so that the Aztecs could capitulate by fleeing. Then they all converged toward the center of the city.

The Spanish remembered how, a year before, the Aztecs had hurled themselves upon them from the balconies of houses, how difficult it had been to fight off the incessant hail of stones and spears, and how careful the Aztecs had been to raise the drawbridges to stop the Spanish troops moving from one place to another. This time it was the Spanish who were in control of communications, and they raised the bridges, swam from ditch to ditch, and burned houses and palaces in order to advance more freely with their cavalry. Canals and ditches were filled with debris and smoothed over. Attacks, retreats, ambushes were all conducted with ferocity, courage, and tenacity. As one side built, the other destroyed, day and night, day in, day out.

The city was quickly cut off. Since food supplies could not reach them, the Aztecs began starving: they were reduced to eating grass, roots, lizards, rats, and boiled insects when they were not drinking the blood of the Tlaxcalans. The exhausted city finally fell on August 13, 1521. The siege was over, but conquest was not yet assured.

How is it that the conquistadors, outnumbered more than "a hundred to one," defeated the Aztecs? Their weapons were one factor, particularly their cannon and arquebuses and their horses. The cannon and arquebuses were cumbersome, not amazingly accurate, and useless when the gunpowder was damp, but the noise and flames were frightening to men who had never seen such weapons. The horsemen were equally important. The Spanish horsemen were careful not to get too close to the Aztecs, who could have seized their lances or pulled them down; instead, the Spanish used their spurs and the horses' speed to avoid the dangers of hand-to-hand combat. But like the guns, the horses did much to demoralize the Aztec soldiers. The steel of the Spanish swords, armor, and arrowheads was also superior to the materials used by the Aztecs, a superiority Cortés used in his favor when arranging his men for battle.

Cortés was a skilled soldier and knew how to make his numbers seem larger than they were. But on many occasions, his numbers really were quite large. Cortés exploited the rivalries and disputes among the native tribes, many of which were only too eager to seek revenge against the Aztec oppressors. Cortés was able to get the precious support of many peoples, including the Chalca, Tepanec, and Tlaxcalan, all of whom were tired of Aztec domination. The conquistadors knew how to divide and conquer.

Cortés also used psychological warfare. Pretending to have direct communication with the gods, he led the natives to believe that the horses went into battle of their own free will, and he deceived the Aztecs by quickly hiding the corpses of any animals killed in the fighting; thus many Aztecs believed horses were immortal.

He also played upon his double identity, for he knew that the Aztecs associated him with the god Quetzalcoatl. Myths said that the god would return to reclaim his kingdom, a return that would end the reign of the Aztecs. In this way Cortés kept the Indians in a state of uncertainty and fear. This also contributed to Montezuma's fatal hesitation.

There was one other factor, perhaps the most important of all. When the Spanish arrived in the New World they brought with them a truly fearful weapon: diseases for which the Indians of Mexico had no resistance. When the Spanish landed in Yucatan they brought with them smallpox, and the Indians began dying of it by the hundreds of thousands. This plague was raging among the Aztecs when Cortés attacked their empire, cutting down their numbers and adding to their demoralization.

Moreover, the Aztecs and Spanish were not fighting the same kind of war. The Spanish were prepared to kill, while the Aztecs tried to take their prisoners alive so that they could be used as sacrifice. So although they were superior in number and were fighting on their own territory, the Aztecs were not able to defeat the Spanish.

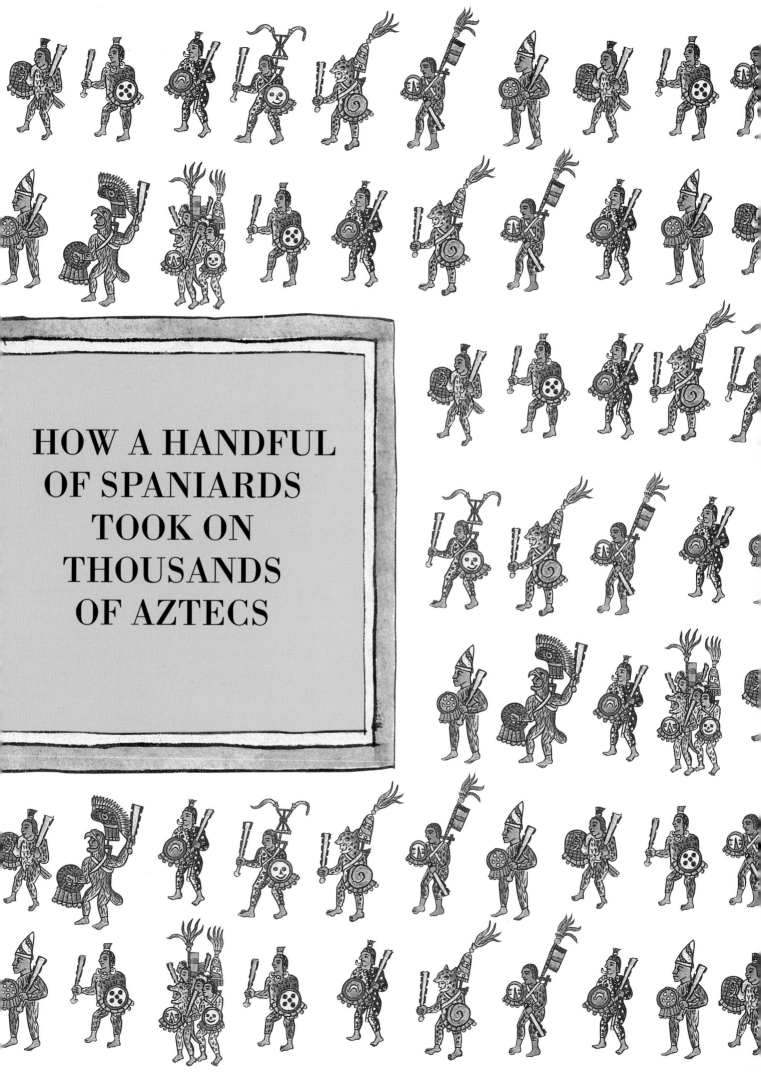

HOW A HANDFUL
OF SPANIARDS
TOOK ON
THOUSANDS
OF AZTECS

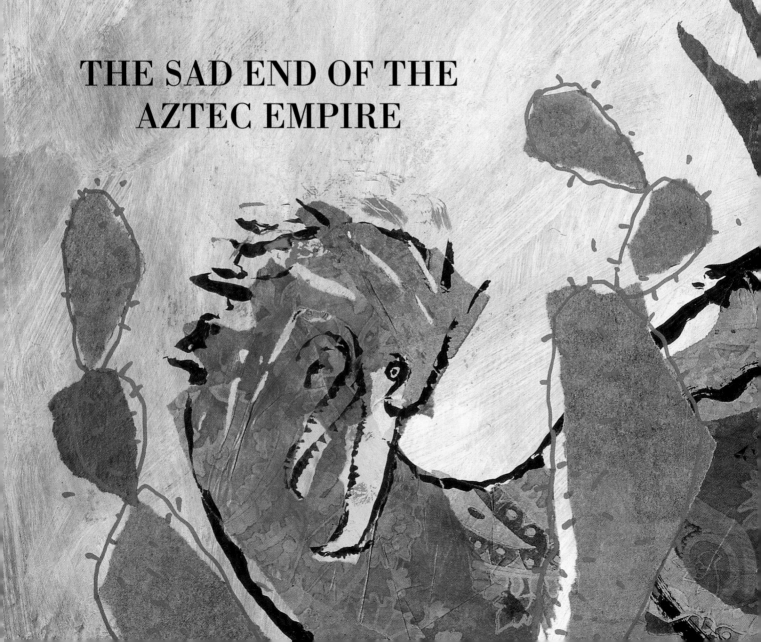

"The fallen eagle" is the name of the last Aztec monarch. Called Cuauhtémoc, he was officially named emperor in January 1521. He had been brought up to be emperor and had been educated in the art of war and in knowledge of religion in the *calmécac* academies, before becoming high priest in the reign of Cuitláhuac. "The features, indeed, the whole person of Cuauhtémoc, gave off an aura of elegance," wrote Bernal Díaz. "He had an elongated, handsome face; when he looked about, his eyes, which were very beautiful, lit up with a soft, gentle, but serious gaze. He was about 22 or 23 then; his skin was lighter than that of most other Indians, who are naturally dark. His wife, a very young and attractive woman, was said to be the daughter of Montezuma, his uncle." Montezuma had been killed during the

Noche Triste in June 1520. His nephew Cuitláhuac had succeeded him, being crowned on September 7 the same year. But the unfortunate young man died of smallpox after a reign of only twenty-eight days. Cuauhtémoc inherited the throne and tried as best he could to fight off the Spanish. But on August 13, 1521, after nineteen months of close cohabitation and three months of bloody warfare, the ravaged city fell to the Spanish. The emperor tried to flee by boat with his family and riches, but was caught by Cortés and his men. "Sir, I have done what I had to do to defend my city and my subjects; I cannot do more, and since fate has made me your prisoner and placed me in your power, take the dagger that you wear at your belt and kill me." However, Cortés did not honor this request, and

THE SAD END OF THE AZTEC EMPIRE

while the conquistadors rebuilt the city and shared out what was left of the Aztecs' wealth, Cuauhtémoc remained a prisoner. He was forced to carry corpses and clear away the ruins of the city, with his feet and wrists in chains. Cortés had now destroyed the Aztec Empire and looked upon himself as the supreme commander and governor of New Spain. In October 1524, he undertook a new expedition to Honduras with Cuauhtémoc. During this voyage, the Aztec prisoner was accused of involvement in a plot and was hanged. The Aztec Empire was at an end. In just a few months, centuries of grandeur and civilization had been destroyed. The empire had been brought down by several factors: the military superiority of the Spanish, who had not only artillery but also cavalry and steel weapons; the cunning skills of Cortés in exploiting the rivalry among the many native tribes; the hesitation and weakness of Montezuma, who after long months of inner doubts had been unable to stand up to Cortés; and finally disease: smallpox and other diseases brought by the Spanish sowed death everywhere, ravaging Tenochtitlán in the autumn 1520.

In a period of less than four years, Cortés had gone from exploring Cuba to destroying the Aztec Empire. On October 15, 1522, Charles V awarded Cortés for his efforts, appointing him commander-in-chief and governor of New Spain, the new name for the land that Cortés had conquered and acquired for the Spanish crown.

These were great days for Spanish conquistadors. But while González de Avila was landing in Honduras (1522), Pizarro setting off for Peru (1524), Bastidas founding Santa Marta in Colombia (1525), and Lucas Vásquez de Ayllón exploring Florida, Cortés was having to prove his innocence. Claims had been made against him that his conquest was not legitimate and that he had wrongfully broken with the authorities in Cuba. The emperor established a royal commission to look into these matters, and in the end Cortés had to speak to Charles V to disprove them. He left Mexico in the spring of 1528 and met the emperor in the autumn in Toledo, Spain. At the end of this visit, he was made marquis of the valley of Oaxaca, meaning owner of a territory in which 23,000 people

CHARLES V CUTS SHORT CORTÉS'

lived, and his duties as commander-in-chief were confirmed. But he was no longer governor: the administration of the new province was given to royal administrators. Six years later, New Spain, now a viceroyalty, was handed over to Antonio de Mendoza.

Although he was now no more than a rich adventurer, Cortés continued to give himself airs: his household included a manservant, two headwaiters, a wine waiter, a pastrycook, a head butler, a majordomo responsible for the gold and silver, a chamberlain, a doctor, a surgeon, two minstrels, three mule drivers, and a dozen pages. When he organized an expedition, he surrounded himself with Spanish captains and important natives; he did not set off without all the servants necessary both for vital necessities and superfluous comforts. He believed this pomp was befitting to his rank, and he knew it helped him impress the natives, who were awed by this imposing figure. He attempted several expeditions along the Baja California coast (1532, 1533, and 1535), which ended badly. He left Mexico for the last time in the spring of 1540, after making gifts of 100 slaves to his legitimate and two illegitimate sons. He had set off from Spain in 1504 at 19 years of age; he returned when he was 55 and died at the age of 62, after having dictated his last will and testament, in which he begged his children to "ease both his conscience and theirs" by treating the Indians with justice. He was buried in Mexico in 1562, as was his dying wish.

CALLING CARD

THE TRUE BRUTALITY
OF THE CONQUEST
AND THE BLACK LEGEND

To prove their invulnerability the conquistadors did not hesitate to use force, even brutality. Their methods were terrifying and cruel and reflected the culture they lived in.

Bartolomé de Las Casas, famous as the apostle of the Indies, denounced the slaughter of Cholula, during which the Spanish summoned all the natives of the city and its environs to a meeting and then "set about massacring or punishing them (as they said) to spread terror in the surrounding countryside at such brutality." They took them prisoner and stabbed them. "After two or three days, we saw Indians, covered with blood, creeping alive out from under the vast number of bodies where they had hidden themselves; they came to beg mercy from the Spanish, asking not to be killed. They received no pity, no mercy; on the contrary, as they came out, they had their throats cut." Las Casas goes on to say that, to make sure their swords were sharp enough, the Spanish would slash the Indians first.

These practices, unfortunately not unique, were used by all those who came to conquer. Some monks complained in a report to the minister of the future Charles V about the way children were being treated in the Caribbean: "Newborn children only have to start crying for the Spanish to seize them by the legs and smash them against the rocks or throw them into the undergrowth, where they die." Arms, legs, noses, breasts, and tongues were cut off; people were torn apart by dogs trained for the purpose; men were burnt alive; the flesh of others was torn off little by little with pincers; women and children were hung up by their feet.

How can we explain such behavior? Was it cruelty, sadistic pleasure? Some of these acts were certainly motivated by the same kind of destructive impulses that we see in other times and other wars. They are demonstrations of the contempt the powerful sometimes show the weak. In most cases, the Spanish tortured the natives to find out where gold was, or to "punish" cannibalism and the practice of human sacrifice, or ignorance of Christianity. In his writings, Las Casas may have sometimes exaggerated the Spanish mistreatment of the Indians in order to get the rulers to stop it, but his works were exploited by Spain's enemies, giving birth to the enduring "Black Legend."

Around the middle of the fifteenth century, the German printer Johann Gutenberg makes a truly important invention: printing with movable type. His first publication, a Bible, appears around 1455.

Engraving is in its infancy, but a collection of prints of fashions, published in 1520, makes "Spanish costume" popular throughout the Hapsburg empire.

Magellan begins his voyage around the world on September 20, 1519; in 1520 he discovers the straits that bear his name; in 1521 he dies in the Philippines, but members of his crew complete the round-the-world voyage in 1522.

1521: Spanish conquistadors found the city of San Juan, Puerto Rico, and use stones brought as ballast in ships to pave the city's streets.

THE LATEST NEWS FROM EUROPE

A new philosophy has appeared: humanism. Its goal is revival of the glories of the ancient world, including Greek and Latin, and it is influential in the coming of the Renaissance.

1523: Turkeys are introduced to Spain and soon reach England. Since no one can pronounce the Mayan word for the birds, uexolotl, they're called turkeys for they're sold by "turkey merchants," who deal in such imported oddities.

Thomas More (1478-1535), English statesman and author, describes an ideal state in Utopia, published in 1516 (the name Utopia means "no place").

The Dutch humanist Erasmus offers personal advice: "To blow your nose on your hat or a flap of your cloak is the mark of a peasant; on your arm or elbow, the mark of a fishmonger. It is not much cleaner to do it into your hand and then wipe it on your clothes; it is much more decent to use a handkerchief." In truth, handkerchiefs are still something of a novelty.

The aristocrats of Renaissance Europe are very fond of exciting spectacles and merrymaking of all kinds. To get the special effects right, theater decor is sometimes set on fire.

The mother of Charles V, Joanna the Mad, likes to surround herself with bears—which live with her in her palace at Ghent in the Netherlands.

Manuel I, king of Portugal and very keen on strange animals, sends off an elephant to Pope Leo X. This animal proceeds to fill its trunk with water from a bucket and douse the assembled company with water. Painters line up to catch its portrait.

The Flemish geographer Gerardus Mercator (1512-94) revolutionizes cartography. He gives his name to the system of map projection that makes use of longitude and latitude.

1512: Houses along a street of Paris are given numbers—the first time this has been done. Notre Dame Bridge Street is given two rows of numbers, one on each side. For the moment, unique to Paris!

1520: England's Henry VIII and France's Francis I meet with 10,000 courtiers for a three-week party known as the Field of the Cloth of Gold. The expense cripples the French treasury. 1522: Henry declares war on France.

1521: "Here I stand," says Martin Luther before the Diet of Worms. "I can't do anything else." Luther's ideas are soon to start a movement that will bring Europe to religious turmoil.

1519: Leonardo da Vinci (1452-1519) dies at Amboise castle on the Loire River in France. Famous as an artist and painter of the Mona Lisa, he is also a sculptor, architect, engineer, writer, and musician.

The slice of bread (or trencher) on which food is served is gradually being replaced by plates made of pewter, silver, or china. This makes meat easier to cut and permits the use of runny sauces.

Europe is discovering the use of the fork. According to some sources, it is first introduced to France by Catherine de' Medici on her marriage, in 1533, to the future king of France Henry II.

1519: A large silver coin is minted in Joachimstal, Bohemia, and is called the Joachimstaler, a word that will soon to shortened to thaler and then, in a farther future, will become dollar.

The Italian artist Michelangelo (1475-1564) paints The Creation of Adam on the ceiling of the Sistine Chapel in the Vatican.

1522: Slaves on the island of Hispaniola take part in a large-scale rebellion, the first of at least 10 that will take place over the next thirty years in Spanish possessions.

1524: Spanish conquistador and would-be conqueror Francisco Pizarro knows of the great accomplishments of Cortés and hopes to do even better. He has heard of a land to the south where people drink from golden cups. He he will soon set off for Peru.

THEIR GOD DEPARTED · THE SPANISH · REMAINED

Altars, chapels, churches, baptism,
and the flames used to burn heretics marked
the first phase of conquest in Mexico. A Christian
vision of the world was imposed on the Aztecs; the
upper ranks of society were targeted first in the belief
that the masses would follow. The monk Sahagún taught
Latin to his Tlatelolco pupils, and high-born Indians
composed epic Latin verse. Scarcely twenty years after the siege
of Tenochtitlán, Mexicans were composing masses. Artists and
illustrators of religious codices mixed Christian and traditional motifs;
young Indians were depicted wearing Spanish clothes, or sitting in Western
chairs, legs crossed; canvas and fresco techniques were used; but in the same
way Aztec calendars appeared on pottery made by Franciscan monasteries. A
new world was being born, a new mixed society was coming into being. Mestizos
(children of a Spanish man and a native Indian woman), castizos (children of a mestizo
and an Indian woman), mulattos (children of a Spaniard and a black woman), and Spanish
(children of two Spaniards or of a castizo man and a Spanish woman) were proof of this. Many
rituals persisted despite the conquest. The Square of Three Cultures in Mexico City still contains
the remains of an Aztec temple, a church in the Spanish Jesuit style, and contemporary architecture.
The Virgin of Guadalupe, the Virgin Mary depicted as an Indian woman, is venerated, but the site of her
worship was sacred before the Spanish conquest as the shrine of the goddess Tonantzin, mother of the
gods. Beneath the new beliefs is the original heritage, a combination that gives Mexico its culture.

Destruction of idols by fire, 1583-85.

IT TAKES MORE THAN PENCILS TO COLOR IN A CULTURE

The Aztecs did not use a phonetic alphabet. Instead they used a system of symbols, or glyphs, that expressed their thoughts, beliefs, and history. The sign of a footprint indicated movement (see page 33), an eye meant sight. These "paintings," later called codices, were done by specialists on deerhide or agave parchment. The whole work, consisting of pictograms, ideograms, and phonetic markers, was folded like an accordion and could measure up to 30 feet in length when opened. The Borgia Codex, which is about religious rites and the astrological calendar, is one of the rare examples that have come down to us from the pre-Columbian era. It is now housed in Rome. What about the others? Most were created after the conquest. In their anxiety to convert the natives, some priests realized how important it was to understand the thinking of their new converts. Some, like the Dominican Diego Duran and the Franciscan Bernardino de Sahagún, conducted what amounts to sociology and ethnology, long before these fields of study were invented. "My only wish is to speak about the Aztec nation, of its achievements and the disastrous fate that led to its undoing," wrote Diego Duran when he published his *Historia de las Indias de Nueva Espana*. The codex written under the supervision of Sahagún presents an extraordinary story: he lived in Mexico from 1529 to 1590, just a few years after the fall of the capital. For decades he collected eye-witness accounts of Aztec civilization. In 1577, Philip II of Spain ordered all such works destroyed. Sahagún's work escaped the flames because he had hidden his notes and sketches. He had almost achieved his aim! Only when he was over 80 was he able to finish the work he had devoted his life to assembling. His work, like that of Duran, was not published until the nineteenth century, by which time people in Europe and Mexico had become interested in this period of history.

INDEX

Acamapichtli, 23
adultery, 24, 27, 38
afterlife, 10-11, 24
Aguilar, Geronimo de, 69
Aiutzotl, 23
Alcolhuas, 9
Alexander VI, Pope, 52
Alvarado, Pedro de, 65, 78, 79, 80
Amantlan, 19
Anahuac, 6
armor, 48-49, 82
arquebus, 48, 64, 82
astrolabes, 51
astrology, 24, 45, 46-47, 95
Axayacatl, 23, 74
Ayllón, Lucas Vásquez de, 86
Aztlán, 9
Bastidas, Rodrigo de, 86
Black Legend, 89
Cabot, John, 59
Cabral, Pedro Alvares, 59
Caesar, Julius, 57
caique, 26
calmécac, 24, 84
calpulli, 26
cannibalism, 21, 89
cannons, 48, 64, 82, 85
Cão, Diogo, 51
Cartier, Jacques, 59
Catalan atlas, 51
Catherine de' Medici, 91
Ceuta, battle of, 51
Chalcas, 9, 82
Charles V, 42, 54-55, 66, 75, 86, 89, 90
Chichimecs, 9
Chicómoztoc, 9
children, 24, 46
Chimalpopoca, 23
Chinampanecas, 9
Cholula, 71, 89
clothing, 28-29
cocoa, 23, 36, 40
Columbus, Christopher, 51, 52, 54, 55, 59, 61, 62, 63
Columbus, Diego, 62
compasses, 51
conquistadors, 56-57, 86, 89
Copernicus, Nicholas, 51
Córdoba, Fernández de, 62
Cortés, Hernán, 42, 46, 54, 59, 60-61, 62, 65, 66, 69, 70, 72, 73, 74-75, 77, 78-79, 80, 82, 86
crossbows, 48, 64
Cuauhtémoc, 49, 84-85
Cuitláhuac, 84
Culhuas, 9
Dias, Bartolomeu, 51
Díaz del Castillo, Bernal, 57, 65, 84
diseases, 82, 85
drunkenness, 27, 38
Duran, Diego, 95
Erasmus, 90
expulsions, 54-55
feathers, 18, 30, 43, 49
Ferdinand, King, 37, 52, 55
food, 19, 21, 23, 40-41
Four Suns, 6
Francis I, 53, 59, 91
Gama, Vasco da, 51
gambling, 27, 28, 45
games, 44-45
garland wars, 13, 21, 30-31
gold, 18-19, 29, 30, 42-43, 45,

57, 72, 73, 89
González de Avila, Gil, 86
Grijalva, Juan de, 62, 66
Guerrero, Gonzalo, 69
Gutenberg, Johann, 90
Henry VII, 59
Henry VIII, 91
Henry the Navigator, 51
hidalgos, 57, 80
Hispaniola, 91
Honduras, 65, 85
horses, 33, 38, 48, 82, 85
Huitziliutl, 23
Huitzilopochtli, 9, 10, 13, 15, 17, 23, 24, 30, 31, 47
humanism, 90
human sacrifice, 6, 12-13, 20-21, 35, 78, 89
ichcahuipilli, 49
icpalli, 23
Incas, 5
Isabella, Queen, 37, 52, 55
Italian Wars, 61
Itzcoatl, 23
jaguar warriors, 29
Jerusalem, 51
Jews, 54-55
Joanna the Mad, 90
John II, King, 51, 59
knives, 19, 20, 49
Las Casas, Bartolomé de, 89
Leo X, Pope, 91
Leonardo da Vinci, 91
Lopez, Martín, 81
Luther, Martin, 91
Machu Picchu, 5
Magellan, Ferdinand, 51, 59, 90
maguey, 21
Manuel I, 91
Marina, Doña, 68-69
marriage, 24, 27, 46
maxtlatl, 24, 28
Mayas, 5
medicines, 34-35
Mendoza, Antonio de, 86
Mercator, Gerardus, 91
merchants, 29, 30, 33, 38, 46
Mexica (Aztecs), 6, 9
Mexico, 5, 6, 9, 13, 33, 38
Mexico City, 6, 17. *See also* Tenochtitlán
Michelangelo Buonarroti, 91
Moctezuma. *See* Montezuma
money, 33, 37, 43
Montezuma I, 23
Montezuma II, 17, 23, 33, 42, 46, 54, 59, 69, 70, 72, 73, 74-75, 76-77, 78-79, 82, 84
moon, 11
More, Thomas, 90
Moslems, 54, 55
movable type, 57, 90
Nahua, 9, 15
Nahuatl (language), 9, 21, 69
Narváez, Pánfilo de, 78-79
New Spain. *See* Mexico
nobility, 26
Noche Triste, 77, 78-79, 80, 84
octli, 38
Omecihuatl, 6
Ometecuhtli, 6
patolli, 45
Peru, 91
peyotl, 35, 38
Philip II, 95

Pizzaro, Francisco, 5, 86, 91
Polo, Marco, 51
priests (Aztec), 21, 24, 28, 29, 31, 38, 75, 84
priests (Catholic), 64, 69, 89, 92, 95
printing, 57, 90
Puerto Rico, 90
pulque, 38
punishments, 24, 27, 38
Quetzalcoatl, 15, 17, 24, 46, 47, 69, 73, 75, 82
rapiers, 48
Reformation, Protestant, 54
religion (Aztec), 10-11, 13, 15, 20-21, 35, 75
requerimento, 57
Sahagún, Bernadino de, 10-11, 92, 95
Sixtus IV, Pope, 55
slaves, 27, 28, 31, 38, 45, 91
smallpox. *See* diseases
soldiers, 26, 28
sorcerers, 35
Spanish Inquisition, 55
spies, 31
Tacuba. *See* Tlacopán
tamales, 21, 24, 40
tecuhtli. *See* nobility
teixocuilanques, 35
telpochcalli, 17, 24
Tenochtitlán, 6, 16-17, 18-19, 23, 28, 30, 31, 33, 71, 73, 74-75, 78, 80-81, 84, 85, 92
teocalli, 20
teonancatl, 38
Tepanecs, 9, 82
tetlacuicuiliques, 35
tetlanocuilanques, 35
Texcoco, 23, 28, 30, 72
Texcoco, Lake, 9, 17, 71, 80
Tezcatlipoca, 15, 21, 29, 36
tilmatli, 28
Tizoc, 23
tlachtli, 45
Tlacopán, 23, 28, 30, 72
Tlahuicas, 9
Tlaloc, 10, 15, 17, 24, 35
Tlaltecutli, 13
Tlatepotzcas, 9
tlatoani, 29
Tlaxcala, 70, 79, 82
Tlazolteotl, 15
tobacco, 19, 23, 40
Toltecs, 9
tonalpouhque, 46
Tonantzin, 92
Tordesillas, Treaty of, 52-53
Torquemada, Tomás de, 55
Totonacs, 70
toys, 33
Triple Alliance, 23, 28, 29, 30
Tula, 9
turkeys, 36, 40, 90
ulli, 36, 45
Underworld. *See* afterlife
Velázquez, Diego de, 62, 65, 66, 70
Verrazano, Giovanni da, 59
Vespucci, Amerigo, 61
wheel, 32-33
Xilonen, 21
Xipe-Totec, 15
Xocoyotzin. *See* Montezuma II

BOOKS FOR FURTHER READING

Baquedano, Elizabeth. *Aztec, Inca, and Maya*. New York: Knopf, 1987.
Berdan, Frances F. *The Aztecs*. Broomall, Pa.: Chelsea House, 1989.
Burrell, Roy. *Moctezuma and the Aztecs*. Chatham, N.J.: Raintree Steck-Vaughn, 1992.
Dawson, Imogen. *Food and Feasts with the Aztecs*. Parsippany, N.J.: Silver Burdett, 1995.
Dineen, Jacqueline. *The Aztecs*. New York: Simon & Schuster, 1992.
Gruzinski, Serge. *The Aztecs: Rise and Fall of an Empire*. New York: Harry N. Abrams, 1992.
Marrin, Albert. *Aztecs and Spaniards: Cortés and the Conquest of Mexico*. New York: Simon & Schuster, 1986.
Thomas, Hugh. *Conquest: Montezuma, Cortés, and the Fall of Old Mexico*. New York: Simon & Schuster, 1993.
Warburton, Lois. *Aztec Civilization*. San Diego: Lucent Books, 1995.
Wood, Tim. *The Aztecs*. New York: Viking, 1992.

ILLUSTRATIONS

PHOTOGRAPHS

PHOTO CREDITS